Helping Your Anxious Child

A Step-by-Step Guide for Parents

Ronald M. Rapee, Ph.D., Susan H. Spence, Ph.D.,
Vanessa Cobham, Ph.D., and Ann Wignall, M. Psych.

NEW HARBINGER PUBLICATIONS, INC.

To our parents

Publisher's Note

This publication is designed to provide accurate and authoritative information in regard to the subject matter covered. It is sold with the understanding that the publisher is not engaged in rendering psychological, financial, legal, or other professional services. If expert assistance or counseling is needed, the services of a competent professional should be sought.

Distributed in the U.S.A. by Publishers Group West; in Canada by Raincoast Books; in Great Britain by Airlift Book Company, Ltd.; in South Africa by Real Books, Ltd.; in Australia by Boobook; and in New Zealand by Tandem Press.

Copyright © 2000 by Ronald M. Rapee
        New Harbinger Publications, Inc.
        5674 Shattuck Avenue
        Oakland, CA 94609

Cover design © 2000 by Poulson/Gluck
Illustrations by Roberta Weir
Edited by Angela Watrous
Text design by Tracy Marie Powell

Library of Congress Catalog Card Number: 99-75286
ISBN 1-57224-191-8 Paperback

New Harbinger Publications' Web site address: www.newharbinger.com

05   04   03

15   14   13   12   11   10   9   8   7

Contents

Introduction

Emily had a secret problem. She was twelve years old and was still afraid of the dark. At night, when the family was asleep, she would often hear strange noises outside and panic, imagining that they were being robbed or that they'd all be murdered while they slept. Emily still kept a night-light on in her room and would often run to her parents' room on particularly bad nights and slip into their bed. She'd never take the garbage out at night or go upstairs alone after dark, and she usually insisted on her parents checking her room before she went to sleep. Because of her fear, which was a secret to everyone except her parents, Emily never accepted invitations to sleep over at friends' houses and found excuses to not go to school camp. Emily's parents had tried to push her to face her fears and sleep in the dark, but she became so upset and they had so many fights that eventually they just gave in to her fears. Now her parents feel frustrated at the limitations that Emily's fear causes both in her own life and for everyone else in the family.

Ten-tear-old Connor had a different problem. He was extremely shy. At home he would talk freely with his family. At school or with strangers, Connor was different. He was terrified that he would do the wrong thing and make a fool of himself. He hated to speak in front of the class. Even though he could play the piano beautifully, he was too scared to perform at the school concert. In the schoolyard he was usually alone, afraid to join in with the other children.

If you're reading this book, the chances are there is a child similar to Emily or Connor in your family. Problems like Emily's and Connor's are common, normal, and quite easily handled. But they can often cause unpleasant and potentially serious interference in children's lives and in the lives of their families.

Fear, worry, and anxiety in children can take many forms. All children experience fears and phobias at particular stages of their lives, and this is a normal part of growing up. For example, we know that infants develop a fear of separating from their mom at the same time they begin to fear strangers and new people. A little later, most children will be scared of the dark and, at some point, many young children begin to imagine monsters under the bed and burglars at the door. In the teenage years, self-consciousness and shyness become a very common and often annoying part of developing maturity. When these fears develop, they're usually just part of the normal developmental process that we all go through. But sometimes, fears and worrying can reach a point where they start to cause a problem for the child. These excessive fears are often temporary and transient, but may still cause such distress that as a parent, you want to help your child hurry through this stage. On the other hand, some children experience fears and worries to a much greater degree than their peers, and some continue to experience fears long after other children their age have outgrown them.

Some fears are very understandable and based on obvious causes. For example, your children may be scared to go to school because they are being bullied; or they may be scared of the dark following a burglary at home. In other cases, the fears and worries that children experience are much harder for parents to understand. For example, the children who worry that they're stupid, even though they may be doing perfectly well in school and elsewhere in life. Or the children who are scared that their mom will be killed in a car accident, though no one they know has ever been in a car accident and their mom always makes sure she picks her children up on time. Or the child who worries about and imagines every possible disaster. In these cases the anxiety may be an entrenched part of the child's personality, and you may feel as though your child has been sensitive and high-strung for all of his or her life.

Many adults believe that childhood is a time of carefree days and no responsibility. It may surprise you to know that in fact, anxiety is the most common problem experienced by children of all ages. Diagnosable anxiety disorders are found in around one in ten children, though less pronounced but still distressing fears can be found in far more. Anxiety and worry affect children of all ages, from infants to adolescents. Girls or boys, rich or poor, brilliant or average—it makes no difference—anxiety can affect anyone. Some parents may think, "So what? Everyone gets nervous sometimes. It doesn't hurt anyone, so why all the fuss?" To some extent, these parents may be right. Anxiety is not as dramatic a problem as a child contemplating suicide or engaged in drug abuse. But anxiety is a sign of real personal suffering—it's not an act or a way of getting sympathy (although in a few cases this can complicate the picture). Anxiety can also cause marked interference in children's lives, reducing their school performance, interfering with friendships, and affecting the whole family. In addition, in some cases, anxiety in childhood can be the beginning of a lifetime of anxiousness that, in severe cases, can lead to the more serious problems we just mentioned—drug and alcohol abuse, depression, and even suicide. If you're a parent with an anxious child, you need not fret or worry excessively—anxiety can be managed—but it's good to be motivated to do something to help your child.

Managing anxiousness and helping your child develop confidence and control in life is much the same no matter what form the anxiety takes. In this book we will describe some of the common types of children's anxieties, increase your understanding of children's anxiety, and teach you how you can help your child master his or her fears. We will discuss all sorts of anxieties—from the minor, temporary fears that many children experience, to the longer, more severe, and invasive problems that can so extensively restrict a child's life. Most importantly, we will describe in detail skills and strategies that you can use to help your child learn to control their fears.

By working through this book you will be able to help your child reduce his or her fears and worries. It's certainly possible to do this by yourself, especially if your child's fears are relatively new and not too severe. But it's impossible for us to anticipate each individual case and explain everything you might need for every possible situation. In addition, while you are the best person to help your child, it's hard for parents to be completely objective with respect to either their own or their child's behavior. For this reason, we strongly urge you to consult a mental health professional while using this book. Seeing a therapist is not a stigma or a sign of weakness. A professional can help teach you the strategies that we cover in this book and apply them to your child's specific needs.

Finding a good therapist is not always easy, especially in certain places. Clinical psychologists are the most likely to be familiar with the strategies that we will cover here and should have the best training to help you and your child. However, other professionals who can be very helpful include school counselors or school psychologists, counselors, psychiatrists, and your general practitioner.

In choosing a therapist, it's important to remember that you are the customer and it's your child and your choice. For this reason, you should ask many questions, both before you begin seeing a therapist and while you're seeing them. Some of the questions you can ask include: "How much experience have you had with this type of problem?" "Are you familiar with the techniques and strategies discussed in this book?" "How much do you charge?" "How many sessions will you need to see us?" and "What sort of treatment plan would you be expecting to follow?"

Some of these questions may not be answerable until after the therapist has conducted a thorough assessment of your child, which generally takes one or two sessions. While every case is different, in general, therapists should be clear and direct with you about the goals of therapy, and they should have a concrete and relatively structured treatment plan. Treatment length will vary a great deal depending on many factors, but a relatively straightforward problem with anxiety should be able to be dealt with in roughly eight to twelve sessions. For therapists who would like further information about dealing with anxious children, we have a companion book written specifically for professionals called *Treating Anxious Children and Adolescents: An Evidence-Based Approach* (New Harbinger).

We'll begin our discussion of anxious children by describing several children who we've seen and who have benefited from these strategies. We'll come back to these children throughout the course of this book and use them to show how each of the techniques can be applied to the real world.

Some Real-Life Anxious Children

Talia

Talia is a typical nine-year-old with a big group of friends and a cheeky streak. She loves rock music, is a member of the school soccer team, and rarely worries about a thing. But Talia is scared of water. She learned to swim when she was five years old, but she's never enjoyed it and has always avoided deep water as much as possible. When her father takes her out beyond where she can stand, she begins to panic, clings tightly to him, and begs him to take her back.

No one can figure out why Talia is afraid of the water—she has never had a bad experience there and has never known anyone who has drowned. Both of her brothers love swimming and surfing. Yet something about the water has always been frightening to Talia and, try as she might, she just can't talk herself out of it. Now that Talia is getting older and starting to go to pool parties and the beach with friends, she is running out of excuses and her swimming phobia is beginning to become a problem.

George

Now that he's twelve years old, George's parents believe that he should be doing a lot of things by himself. But George has little self-confidence and worries a great deal about what other people think of him. He has always been a nervous, sensitive, and shy child and grew up having very few friends. Since beginning high school this year, George has retreated even more into his shell. It took him most of the year to make his first friend, Tony, who is also a bit of an outsider. In class, George's teachers report that he rarely says a word and that he becomes very upset if he is asked to answer a question or speak in front of the class. At home, George is quite talkative with his family, but becomes quiet if anyone he doesn't know well comes over. George has very specific rules about what clothes he can and cannot wear, he will always get his parents to deal with shopkeepers and cashiers, and he will never answer the telephone. Despite his parents' urging, George has never joined a club or team and spends most of his time at home alone, building models. From time to time, George talks about feeling lonely and he has gone through a few periods of feeling quite down and miserable.

Lashi

Lashi is a seven-year-old girl whose parents separated two years ago. Since the separation, Lashi has begun to worry a great deal about her mother. She's terrified that her mother will be killed in a car accident or by a burglar and that she will never see her mom again. Lashi cries whenever her mother leaves her and she refuses to be left alone with a baby-sitter or even to sleep over at her grandmother's place. As a result, Lashi's mother has hardly been out since the separation. She is beginning to lose her friends and has no chance to meet other men. Sometimes Lashi is willing to stay overnight with her father, but she always spends the whole time asking about her mother, and lately she hasn't been willing to stay with him at all. It is also a real struggle every morning to get Lashi to go to school, and sometimes Lashi's mother gives in and takes a day off work to let her stay at home. Lashi also worries about burglars breaking into the house and is scared of the dark. Over the past few weeks, she has begun to sleep in her mother's bed, something her mother has allowed, because it is just too much of a struggle to argue. Lashi's mother loves her daughter very much, but lately she has really begun to get fed up with the limitations on her life and is starting to feel angry and resentful.

In addition to her main anxiety, Lashi also has a fear of injections, doctors, and hospitals. Most of the time, this is not a big problem, but occasionally, it makes it very difficult for Lashi to go to the doctor's for treatment and even to visit a sick friend. Having shots is the biggest problem—Lashi missed her last vaccination because she would not allow the nurse to give her an injection.

Kurt

Ten-year-old Kurt is a worrier. He worries about his schoolwork, he worries about his parents' health, and he worries that he will forget to feed his dog and she will starve. Kurt's parents no longer let him watch the evening news because he spends the next two days worrying about all the tragic stories he has seen. They also often don't tell him about new things that he is going to have to do until the very last moment, because when they do, he pesters them mercilessly with his constant questions about what is going to happen. This interrogation also happens whenever Kurt has to do something he finds unpleasant, such as take a test at school or go to the dentist. Kurt will ask his parents for information and reassurance hundreds of times.

Kurt also worries about germs. He's scared when he touches certain things that germs have gotten onto his hands and that he will get sick and die. He worries about infections and all sorts of illnesses. As a result of his worries, Kurt washes his hands again and again all day long. For example, after going to the bathroom, Kurt will scrub his hands for several minutes. He will also rush off to wash whenever he has touched something he thinks may be contaminated, such as public door handles and seats where other people have been sitting. Kurt refuses to go to certain places, such as hospitals or the cafeteria at his school, because of the germs he thinks are there. He will sometimes get particular ideas about things that are contaminated that will then become taboo. For example, he went through a phase of avoiding the back garden because the dog had once thrown up there. Last week, Kurt caught the train with his mother and they sat opposite a man who sneezed several times. When he got home, Kurt raced straight to the shower and washed for forty-five minutes.

These children show just some of the ways that anxiety can affect a child's life. There are many types of anxiety and many ways that children can show its effects. In fact, the forms that children's worries can take are as varied as the number of children themselves. As you can see, fears do not always have to be "weird" or "crazy." Many normal and common types of concerns can become a problem for children if they interfere with something they want or need to do. Fears and worries can also clearly vary in their intensity and effects.

The good news is that problems such as these can be managed very well. In the rest of this book we will describe the skills including relaxation, thinking realistically, facing up to fears, and learning better social interaction. Each skill will be described in detail, examples and forms will be provided, and we will apply the concepts to the cases of children we've introduced. Finally, we will discuss the future, what you can do to help your child maintain his or her gains and what to do if problems reemerge. Throughout the program your child will not only be building his or her confidence, but will also be earning rewards and time with you and the rest of your family. In our experience, most children going through this program have a great time and find the whole experience fun and exciting while they learn to overcome their fears and worries.

Chapter 1

Why Is Your
Child Anxious?

Chapter Objectives

In this chapter you will learn:

- how to recognize if your child can use help
- some of the forms that anxiety can take in children
- some ideas about the possible causes of anxiety in children
- how these causes will be addressed by the treatment program

Normal Fears

Fears are a normal and natural part of life. They're part of our evolution as a species, and they emerge and develop at specific times in our lives. Fear of strangers and fear of separating from the main caregiver will typically show up in children at around nine months of age. Naturally, the exact age and the amount of fear will vary slightly from child to child, but all children will go through these fears and most show up at similar times. As children get older, they'll begin to show other natural fears. Fear of animals (e.g. dogs) and insects (e.g. spiders) fear of the water, fear of the dark, and fears of the supernatural (e.g. ghosts and monsters) often start to show up in young children in the toddler years and beyond. Around middle to late childhood, children begin to be more aware of other children and will begin to become self-conscious and develop a strong desire to fit in. These worries usually increase over the following years and peak in midadolescence, when how a teen looks and what the other kids think of him or her become the most important things in the world.

When Does Anxiety Become a Problem?

How do you decide if your child's fear is "abnormal"? Quite simply, you don't! There is no such thing as an "abnormal fear." All fears are normal—some are simply more intense and more extensive than others. Even fears that might at first appear strange, such as a fear of germs that causes a child to wash a lot, can simply be seen as normal fears that have gotten too extreme. After all, most people worry at least a little about germs—just ask yourself if you would eat dinner out of your dog's bowl! So children with anxiety problems can simply be thought of as having normal worries that have become more extreme and more intrusive than those of other children.

A better way to think about these things is to consider whether your child's anxiety is a problem for him or her. Does it interfere with or cause difficulties for your child? These difficulties may be many and varied. For example, it may simply be that your child's fears cause your child to be upset and distressed. Or they may stop your child from doing things that he or she likes. Or it may be that worrying is affecting your child academically or in athletic pursuits.

The bottom line is that if your child's anxiety is adversely affecting his or her life, then you may want to consider helping your child to overcome it. The final decision will depend on the balance between how much the anxiety is affecting your child and how much effort you, your child, and the rest of your family are willing to put into working on the fear. The decision has to be made not only by yourself, but also by your child. It may be that you and your child will decide that while he or she is somewhat affected by anxiety, the time is not right or the problem is not troublesome enough to necessitate working on it. On the other hand, you may decide that even though the anxiety doesn't seem to be such a big problem, working on it together would be fun, and it would be nice to be rid of it.

In making a decision, you should remember that working on the strategies described in this book takes dedication, hard work, and commitment. But it can also be enjoyable. The activities aren't in any way harmful or dangerous, and they usually reap many additional benefits, such as improved self-esteem, confidence, and general happiness.

How Common Are Anxiety Problems?

As we mentioned in the introduction, so-called anxiety disorders are the most common type of psychological problem found in children and adolescents. Approximately one in ten children meets the criteria for what is technically called an anxiety disorder. The particular disorders vary somewhat with age. Fears of separating from caregivers is more common at younger ages, while social fears are more common at older ages.

Interestingly, even though anxiety disorders are so common in the real world, they are not the most common problem in child mental health clinics. Mental health centers for children are much more likely to see children with aggressive difficulties, attentional difficulties, eating disorders, or suicidal tendencies. What seems to be happening is that even though anxiety is common in children, most parents don't think of taking their anxious child to a professional for help. This may be because parents believe that anxiety is simply a part of their child's personality and there is nothing they can do about it. Or it may be because anxiety doesn't affect parents or teachers as much as these other problems, and so they don't realize how much the anxiety is affecting the child. In addition, in many areas mental health services for children are more prepared and used to dealing with aggression problems than with anxiety. As a result, parents often feel that they are making "mountains out of mole hills" in worrying about their child and may be discouraged from seeking help.

How Does Anxiety Affect Children?

Overall, anxiety doesn't have as dramatic an impact on a child's life as problems like drug use or delinquency. But problems with anxiety can still affect a child's life to quite an extent.

Anxious children tend to have fewer friends than other children their age. Because many anxious children are shy, they have difficulty meeting new children and joining clubs and groups. For this reason, they often have a limited number of friends, and they may not interact with their friends as much as other children. In turn, lack of friendships can have an important impact later in life, increasing loneliness and reducing the opportunity for peer support.

Anxiety can also affect a child's academic achievements. Many anxious children do very well at school because their conscientiousness and perfectionism make them try harder. But they may not be doing as well as they could. This is especially the case for those children who worry a great deal. We often find that these children delay homework and struggle with their lessons, not because they are incapable, but because their worry stops them from approaching the tasks confidently. Shy children may also get less out of the class and the teacher because their anxiety stops them from making full use of the resources (e.g. they may not ask questions in class). In addition, many anxious children may do well in the classroom situation, but fail when it comes to exams because their worry about failing stops them from being able to concentrate. In the longer run, research has shown that shy children have more restricted choices and opportunities in terms of careers. Many careers (e.g. sales, media, or legal work) may be out of the question for shy adolescents because of their worry about performing in front of others.

While many anxious children will change as they grow and mature and may well become confident, outgoing adults, some will develop into anxious adults. Anxiety disorders in adulthood can be a serious hindrance in life. Anxious adults are more likely to abuse drugs and alcohol, miss work or be unemployed, have illnesses and visit a variety of medical specialists, and be depressed and even suicidal. We aren't trying to suggest that this will happen to your child. But even if the effects of anxiety for your child are at the mild end—perhaps a few missed opportunities—it would be better to do something now than wait to see if more severe problems develop.

What Does Anxiety in Children Look Like?

Everyone is individual and no two anxious children will behave exactly the same. But there are some broad similarities that we can describe.

When children experience anxiety, they're likely to notice it affecting them in three ways. First, anxiety is experienced in the mental processes or thoughts that they have. Anxious children will have thoughts that center around some type of danger or threat. For example, they may worry that they'll be hurt, that someone close to them may be hurt, or that they'll be laughed at. Second, anxiety is experienced physically in the body. When a child becomes anxious, his or her body becomes more "pumped up" or aroused. Researchers often refer to this as the fight-or-flight response because its purpose is to help protect the person by preparing them to combat or escape potential danger. The fight-or-flight response includes changes such as rapid heart rate, increased breathing, sweating, and nausea. Therefore, when worried, anxious children may complain of stomachaches, headaches, vomiting, diarrhea, or tiredness. Third, and probably most importantly, anxiety affects children's behavior. When children are anxious, they may fidget, pace, cry, cling, or shake. In addition, anxiety usually involves some type of avoidance. This may be obvious avoidance (e.g. refusing to take the garbage out in the dark) or it might involve more subtle avoidance (e.g. helping all night with the music at a party so they don't have to talk to anyone).

The amount of anxiety will vary from child to child. Some children are afraid of simply one or two things. For example, a child may be generally confident and outgoing but simply be scared of going to sleep with the light out. At the other end of the spectrum, some children may be worried about many areas of life and may seem generally nervous or sensitive. For example, a child may worry about any new situation; be scared to meet new children; be afraid of dogs, spiders, and the dark; and worry about his or her parents going out at night.

There are also certain common anxiety patterns that we see time and again and we will describe these in the following sections.

Specific Phobias

Specific phobias are fears of particular objects or situations. A child with a specific phobia is afraid of a particular thing, such as the dark. Some common specific phobias include the dark, dogs, heights, spiders, storms, and injections. Talia, who we introduced earlier, has a specific phobia of water.

Separation Anxiety

Separation anxiety is the fear of being away from a main caregiver, most commonly, a child's mother. Children with separation anxiety become very upset when they have to separate from their main caregiver for any reason. In severe cases they may follow the parent from room to room so as not even to be out of their parent's sight. More commonly, these children will avoid going to school, get upset when their parents try to go out, refuse to sleep over at other people's houses, and try to keep their parent(s) with them at all times. Some children will report stomachaches or other physical problems when they separate and many will throw tantrums when separation is threatened. The reason for this behavior seems to be a fear that something terrible will happen to the parent or the child while they are apart, and that they consequently will never see each other again. Lashi, who we introduced earlier, developed separation anxiety after her parents were separated.

Generalized Anxiety

Generalized anxiety is a general tendency to be worried or anxious about many areas of life. These children are often described by their parents as worrywarts. They worry about many general problems such as health, schoolwork, sport performance, bills, burglaries, and even their parents' jobs. They're particularly concerned about any new or novel situation they have to face and will often go to their parents repeatedly to ask questions and seek reassurance. Many parents report that television shows such as the evening news or police dramas will send their child into a fit of worrying for days. Kurt, who we introduced earlier, has generalized anxiety in addition to his main problem of obsessive-compulsive disorder.

Social Anxiety or Social Phobia

Social anxiety or social phobia is the fear and worry in situations where the child has to interact with other people or be the focus of attention. These children are more commonly described as shy, and the central problem is a fear that other people will think badly of them in some way. As a result, they may avoid many situations that necessitate interaction with other people, including meeting new people, talking on the telephone, joining teams or clubs, answering questions in class, or wearing the "wrong" clothes. George, who we introduced earlier, has social anxiety.

Obsessive-Compulsive Disorder

Obsessive-compulsive disorder is likely present when there are certain actions or thoughts that the child repeats over and over again, often for long periods. Children with obsessive-compulsive problems may have particular thoughts or themes that play on their mind again and again. For example, they may worry about dirt or germs continuously, or they may continually be worried about keeping order and neatness. In addition, these children will usually perform some actions repeatedly, often in a superstitious or ritualistic way. For example, they may wash repeatedly in a particular pattern for long periods of time, or they may organize and reorganize their belongings in a very specific pattern. Kurt's main problem is one of obsessive-compulsive disorder.

Some children with obsessive-compulsive disorder may have quite complex and involved problems. At times, these problems can be combined with tics and neurological problems, as well as sometimes quite extreme and unusual behaviors. We have previously suggested that it is most effective to try to help your anxious child together with the help of a therapist, but this is especially the case if your child has obsessive-compulsive disorder.

Panic Disorder

Panic disorder is a fear or worry about having panic attacks. Panic attacks involve a sudden rush of fear that comes together with a number of physical feelings (i.e. racing heart, sweating, dizziness, tingling, and breathlessness). During a panic attack, children may believe that they are dying or that something terrible is happening to them. Panic disorder is not common in young children and is more likely to be found in older adolescents. Sometimes these adolescents will begin to avoid many situations because of their panic attacks and, in these cases, the problem is referred to as panic disorder with agoraphobia.

Rosanne was fifteen when she experienced her first panic attack. She was at a friend's party when she began to feel dizzy and sick. Her eyes became blurry and everything seemed to be happening from a long way off. Rosanne was convinced she was going to faint and yelled at her friends to call an ambulance. Many medical tests failed to find any physical problems, but from that time, Rosanne began to be very afraid of any situations that caused strange feelings in her body such as flickering lights, fairground rides, or even exercise. Rosanne continues to have panicky feelings from time to time and is now starting to restrict her life so that she does not put any strain on her body.

Post-Traumatic Stress Disorder

Post-traumatic stress disorder is a reaction to a serious traumatic event in which the child was extremely afraid or injured. Events that might trigger such reactions include car accidents, natural disasters, sexual abuse, or being involved in a robbery. Most children will show some anxiety for a few weeks after a traumatic event. Usually, this reaction gradually disappears. In some cases, the reaction continues for many months. They may keep remembering the event or have bad dreams about it, perhaps even including the trauma in their play. They may suddenly act or feel as if the event is happening again and become very upset. They will often try hard to avoid situations that remind them of the trauma and may become distant in their feelings. They may show jumpiness, sleep difficulties, and irritability.

Danny is nine years old. Six months ago he and his father were involved in a car accident. They were stopped at the head of a line of cars waiting at the traffic lights on a busy main road. All of a sudden, the driver of a car coming toward them lost control of his vehicle. Danny watched in terror as the car came toward him and crashed straight into the front. He felt utterly helpless. Although he has since recovered physically from the accident, the emotional impact of the accident on Danny remains severe. Danny is often irritable and throws tantrums regularly, something he never did before. Many nights, he wakes in fright as he relives the terror of the accident in his dreams. He is frightened of traveling in cars and often panics when stopped at traffic lights on busy intersections.

As with obsessive-compulsive disorder, children with post-traumatic stress disorder sometimes have quite specific and specialized needs in terms of help. For this reason, it's especially important to seek the help of a qualified expert if your child suffers from post-traumatic stress disorder.

What Causes Anxiety in Children?

No one knows the complete answer to this question. But research has identified a number of factors that are likely to play a role in some way. The following sections discuss some of the identified causes of anxiety in children.

Genetics

There is little doubt that anxiety runs in families. People who are anxious can often identify some close relative who also seems to be an anxious person, and it's pretty common for at least one parent of anxious children to also be somewhat anxious. In some cases, this might involve a serious level of anxiety, while in others it might simply be a parent who tends to worry a little more than average. This is particularly likely to be seen in children with higher levels of anxiety. Children with only a specific phobia of one situation are much less likely to have anxious parents.

Research has shown that what is passed on from parent to child is not a specific tendency to be shy or worry about the dark, but a general personality that is more emotionally sensitive than other people's. Just as people vary in how tall they are or the color of their hair, people vary in how generally emotional they are. Genetically, anxious children tend to have a personality that is more emotional than the average. On the positive side, this means that they are likely to be more caring, kind, honest, and loving. But on the negative side, this emotionality means that they are more likely to worry, brood, feel down, and be fearful. There are both positives and negatives to any child's personality, and we can't and don't want to change these. But the techniques in this book *will* show you how to adjust some of the things that really interfere with your child's life.

Parent Reaction

The way you react to or handle your children might also play some role in the development of their anxiety. While all parents differ, it seems that some parents react to their anxious children in an overly protective way. This is very understandable. Parents love their children, and so when faced with a child who is scared, vulnerable, and worried, parents only too naturally rush to their aid. But, in some cases, this helping behavior may become too much of a pattern. Some parents begin to anticipate their child's anxiety and will start to help their child even when it isn't necessary. This is especially the case if the parents themselves are also anxious. If this pattern becomes established, the child isn't forced to face his or her

learned helplessness

fears, and as a result may begin to learn that "the world really is dangerous" and "I cannot handle it myself."

Some parents might also accidentally reward their child's anxious behaviors by paying a great deal of attention to them when they occur. As we will discuss later, it's important not to make too big a fuss over your child's anxiety so that he or she does not get the reward of extra attention. During this program, you will learn to empathize with your child about his or her fears and then encourage him or her to do something positive about it in a calm and consistent manner.

Modeling

There's little doubt that children copy their parents. Just think of the young girl who walks out of her mom's room covered in makeup and wearing high heels and jewelry. It is reasonable, then, to expect that children may also copy their parents' ways of coping with the world. If a parent is anxious and copes by avoiding situations, then the child may learn that this is the way to handle fears. We're not saying that you're entirely responsible for your child's anxiety, and there is no way that modeling could explain even the majority of anxious behaviors. But if your child already has some anxious tendencies and either you or your partner are anxious, your child may pick up a few of these behaviors, and this may further impair their already anxious nature.

Stressors

When a child is bitten by a dog, they will become wary of dogs for a period of time. When a child's parents separate and divorce, the child will often lose some confidence and become more sensitive for a time. These are natural responses that happen to children. If a child experiences stressors like these and is already sensitive and anxious, then these stressors may have an even bigger impact than usual and may add to their anxiety. Common stressors include parental separation, family violence, death of a loved one, being bullied at school, doing badly in school, getting sick, and specific incidents (e.g. being in a car accident, being burgled, being bitten or stung, and being in a fire). Experiences like these cannot be identified in all or even the majority of cases of anxiety. But they may be important in triggering anxiety in some children.

How Do You Help Your Anxious Child?

As you can see, there are many pathways and possible causes of anxiety in children. There is little point in worrying about these causes because in most cases, the initial causes of anxiety in a child are either not directly changeable (e.g. their genes) or they are in the past (e.g. a stressful event). Luckily, it is possible to learn to master anxiety without having to change the original cause. The answers to this can be found by looking at what maintains the anxiety. In other words, what keeps the anxiety going when the cause or trigger (i.e. a stressful event) is over.

Based on a large amount of research, we now believe that a child's anxiety is kept going through several factors. These include the way the child thinks (anxious children see the world as generally dangerous), the way the child copes with his or her fears (anxious children tend to run away from frightening situations), and the way that you and your child interact (many parents learn to take over for their anxious child). All of these factors are possible to change or alleviate, and you will learn how to do this during this program.

In Summary

To summarize, anxious children believe that the world is a dangerous place. Because of this belief, they will often interpret very innocent events as examples of danger. For example, a normal noise outside at night might be interpreted as a burglar. In this way, this thinking style can help to maintain anxiety by seemingly giving the child evidence to support his or her fears. Similarly, anxious children will usually avoid things they fear. Because of this avoidance, they never find out that what they were scared of probably won't happen. Again, this maintains anxiety by not allowing them to discover contrary evidence. When parents allow their children to avoid their anxieties by doing things for them and protecting them from possible worry, parents are allowing these beliefs to stay in place.

In this book, we will help you teach your child how to think more realistically about the world and expect less danger in situations; we will teach you different ways of handling and interacting with your child; and we will show you how you can encourage your child to approach the situations he or she fears in a gradual and consistent manner. Together with these strategies, we will also cover some additional techniques that may be of help in some circumstances. We will go through relaxation with your child to give them a concrete way of coping with tension, and we will discuss some other coping strategies, such as improved social skills, assertiveness, and dealing with teasing.

In the following table, we've listed some of the common factors that might help to keep your child feeling anxious. Next to each, we have listed the techniques that we will be helping you teach your child to combat each of these anxiety factors. It's the combined package of these techniques that will be most effective in teaching your child to beat his or her fears.

Maintaining Factor	Helping Technique
Extreme thinking	Realistic thinking
Difficulty coping	Relaxation
Protective parenting	Child management skills
Avoidance behaviors	Reality testing
Difficulty interacting with others	Social skills
Being pushed around	Assertiveness

Not all of these strategies will be necessary for each child. Generally, the broader and more general the problem, the more strategies will be necessary. With more specific and simple fears, only one or two techniques may be sufficient (particularly the systematic approach to situations, called reality testing, discussed in chapter 6). The particular techniques you end up relying on will be up to you and your child. But we think you will find these techniques to make sense, to be practical, and to help your child to master his or her fears. We describe some sample programs in chapter 8.

Chapter 2

How Do Thoughts and Feelings Affect Anxiety?

Chapter Objectives

In this chapter you will learn:

- some ways to help get your child started on the program
- how to teach your child to understand and recognize anxious feelings
- how to help your child understand how anxiety affects the body
- how to help your child recognize anxious thoughts

Motivating Your Child to Begin This Program

It can be difficult to get anxious children to try anything new. Usually they tend to expect the worst and feel apprehensive at the thought of having to do something that they haven't tried before. They may worry that the program will be too difficult or that they'll be forced to do frightening things that they feel they can't do. Many anxious children also like to try to appear perfect in front of their parents, and so may have difficulty admitting their limitations. At the same time, your child is probably aware of how uncomfortable it feels to be anxious and would most likely prefer to be free of anxiety.

Working through the anxiety-management exercises in this book will require hard work and dedication. Therefore, it's important to have your child's full cooperation. More than that, he or she will need to be motivated to change.

A good way to encourage your child's cooperation and motivation is to discuss the negative aspects of being anxious and the benefits that might come from learning to control anxiety. Together with your child, begin by writing a list of the ways in which anxiety interferes with his or her life. In other words, what does anxiety stop him or her from doing and in what ways does it feel bad? Use the space provided. You can include such things as interference with friends, schoolwork, sport, clubs, and outings. Or you can include that anxiety causes fear, sadness, crying, and fights. Making such a list can show children how their fears and worries are bossing them around, controlling their life.

Being anxious makes me . . .	Being anxious stops me from . . .
When I am not anxious I will feel . . .	When I am not anxious I will be able to . . .

The next step is to make another list, this time of ways in which your child's life will be different when he or she is no longer afraid. What are the things he or she will be able to do? Where will he or she be able to go? How will he or she feel? Again, we have provided a space for this list, or you can write on a board or large sheet of paper. It's a good idea for your child to decorate the final version of this list and paste it someplace where you and your child can see it throughout the program.

Remember that this program will not take away all the normal protective anxieties that any child may have in certain situations (e.g. being scared of walking down a dark alley). Instead, it aims to teach skills to manage the excessive anxiety that is stopping your child from doing things that they see other children doing and that he or she would like to be able to do as well.

You might also like to discuss with your child any fears he or she may have about doing this program. Some of the important points to cover include:

- Feeling anxious is normal and there are many other kids who feel just the same.

- You and your child will work on this program together—you are included every step of the way.

- Your child will not be forced to do anything he or she doesn't want to do.

- New skills will be learned one small step at a time.

- The program will be fun, and it will also include rewards that can be earned.

Getting the Most Out of the Program

As you work through the program, you will see that each step includes several different forms or worksheets for you and your child to fill in. We have included these because, in our experience, this is the best way for children and parents to keep track of their goals for the week. To get the most out of the program it's very important that your child regularly completes these worksheets. Reward your child for his or her efforts in completing the worksheets by consistently showing encouragement and interest in what he or she has written. Most children appreciate stamps, small stickers, or tokens that they can cash in for bigger rewards. Giving your child a star or sticker each time he or she successfully completes a form or exercise is a good way to help make the program fun and to motivate your child to continue. However, attention and interest from you as well as your praise will be the most powerful rewards and the best ways to motivate your child. We will say more about using rewards later.

Learning about Feelings

Many children have difficulty in naming feelings and in being able to describe the differences between various emotional states. Making sure that your child understands different emotions and the ways that emotions are similar or different is an important step before moving on to teach ways of controlling anxiety.

We've included a number of faces on the following page showing different types of expressions. Show your child the pictures and ask them to describe how that person is feeling. There are no right answers—the aim is to help your child identify a range of different feelings. It might be a fun game to get your child to make faces for different emotions. If the rest of the family is willing to get involved, you can make a set of cards or pieces of paper with different feelings written on them, and have each person take turns in picking one of the cards and acting out that feeling without using words. Other members of the family can then try to guess as quickly as possible what the feeling is.

For older children, you might describe a series of different situations (e.g. winning a prize, losing a wallet, etc.) and get them to say how they would feel in that situation. You can make a game of trying to get your older child to come up with as many different words to describe similar feelings as possible (e.g. anxious, nervous, shy, worried, etc.).

The Worry Scale

The next step is to teach your child how to measure his or her feelings. This is important to help your child understand that strong emotions do not just come from nowhere or "out of the blue." In addition, being able to distinguish between different levels of fear will be very important later in the program.

We use the worry scale to show different degrees or levels of anxiety. The thermometer uses a scale from 0 to 10, on which different levels of anxiety are marked from 0 (very relaxed) to 10 (very

How Are You Feeling Today?

Instructions: Label the emotion shown by each face below: sad face, worried face, angry face, scared face, relaxed face

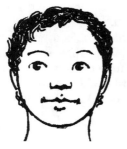 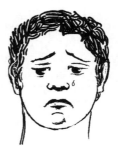

 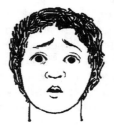

Figure 2.1   Labeling Different Feelings

worried). This is a personal judgment; everyone will have different perceptions for different situations. What is important is that your child learns to recognize that anxiety is not an "all-or-none" feeling, but can actually vary in degree.

Show your child the worry scale and explain the overall scheme. Then ask him or her to show you what numbers would best describe his or her degree of worry in different situations. Some situations might include playing with a friend, seeing a small or large dog, being in bed with the light off, having to give a talk at school, or seeing a large spider on the wall.

In order to practice and get into the habit, it is a good idea to ask your child how anxious he or she is in different situations through the day. This will help your child to become more aware of his or her anxiety levels and will also give the two of you a common language to use to describe his or her anxiety (e.g. "I feel at 4 now," or "I'm a 7 at the moment").

How Anxiety Affects Your Child

In the previous chapter, we described for you how anxiety can affect a person. We discussed the idea that anxiety affects three different aspects of a person—their body, behavior, and thoughts. It's also important for your child to develop an understanding of this lesson by becoming aware of how anxiety affects him or her.

How Anxiety Affects the Body

When we become frightened, our body goes through many changes, including increased heart rate, changes in breathing, sweating, shaky legs, muscular tension, and various other reactions. You can begin to get your child to think about these changes by asking him or her to think of frightened animals, such as a cat. Ask what physical changes would happen if a cat was asleep and woke up suddenly to see a dog standing next to it (e.g. fur standing up, big eyes, tensed body, and scared expression). Next, ask your child to think about how his or her own body feels during anxious times. A good way to do this is to have your child draw the parts of his or her body that are affected by fear or worry. We have included an outline of a body that your child can use to show where anxiety affects him or her. You may choose to enlarge this picture on a photocopier so your child can decorate it and hang it up. A fun alternative is to get

How are you feeling today?

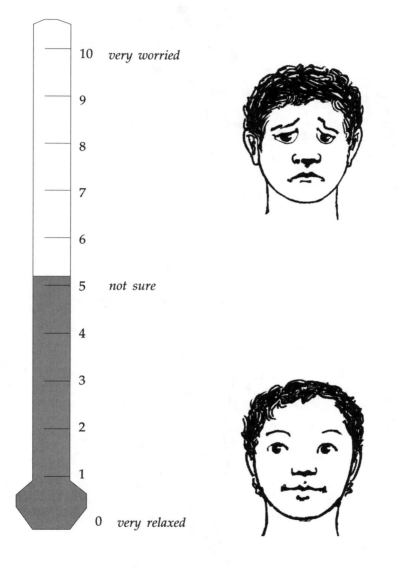

Figure 2.2   Worry Scale

Instructions: Circle or draw an arrow to changes which happen in your body when you are nervous.

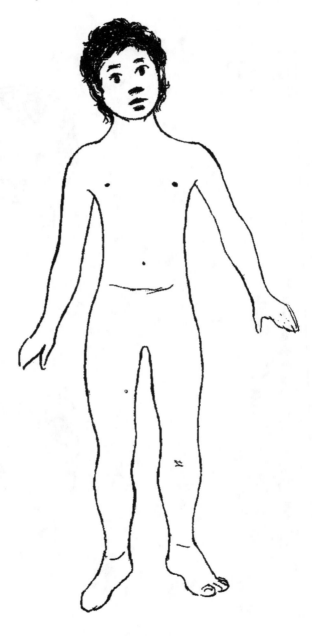

Figure 2.3   How Does My Body Feel When I Am Worried?

a huge sheet of paper and have your child lie on it. Then draw an outline of your child with a pen on the paper. Your child can then use this personal "portrait" to color and show where and how anxiety affects him or her.

How Anxiety Affects Thoughts

It's also important for your child to become more aware of his or her worried thoughts and beliefs. Your child will learn through this program that certain feelings go along with certain thoughts and that anxious feelings tend to go with thoughts of danger. In addition, he or she needs to begin to become more aware of the particular bad things that he or she tends to expect.

We have included a number of cartoons that show different feelings. Show each one to your child and ask him or her to say what thought might come up in each situation. Try to get your child to suggest thoughts that indicate some sort of event rather than simply describing the feeling. For example, a thought such as "this is going to hurt" is good because it describes a bad outcome that the person might be expecting while waiting anxiously for an injection (as opposed to a thought such as "I am scared," which simply describes the feeling before anything has occurred). One of the potentially

Figure 2.4

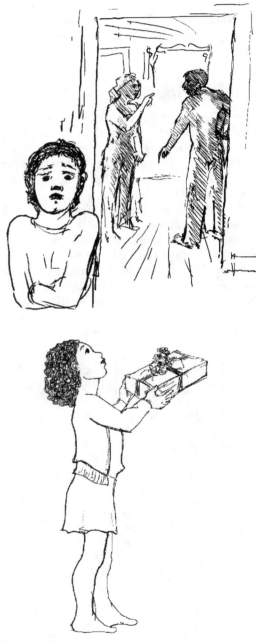

Figure 2.4   *(continued)*

hardest things for children in this part of the program is to learn the difference between thoughts and feelings, so it is best to try not to confuse these things. You might want to point out to your child that feelings such as fear, worry, shyness, or anxiety are connected with negative thoughts that we call "worried thoughts." The concept of worried thoughts will become important in the next chapter.

The next step in the program is to help children understand that there is a link between a situation, their thoughts, and how they are feeling. To do this, you can describe some situations to your child and ask him or her to tell you what she or he would be thinking and feeling. In this way you can start to show your child that certain thoughts and feelings are linked. You can use the "linking thoughts and feelings" form that we have included. Make several copies so you can give a number of examples. Following is an example of how to complete this form:

Start by asking your child to think of a time when they felt really happy and relaxed. Ask him or her to think about where they were, whom they were with, and what they were doing. Briefly describe the situation in the first box on the form. Now, ask your child to try to remember what they were thinking or saying to him- or herself in his or her head. This might be a bit hard to remember if the situation happened a long time ago. If they can't remember exactly what they were thinking, try to guess what one might have been thinking in the situation. Write this in the "What was I thinking" box. Then, ask your child to indicate how they were feeling. Write this in the "What was I feeling" box. Finally, have your child rate how strong the feeling was using the scale.

Next, repeat the above exercise thinking of a time when your child felt really worried or afraid. Remember, the key is practice so make more copies of this form and try and repeat the exercise using several other situations.

How Anxiety Affects Behavior

It's a good idea to also get your child to think about how he or she behaves or acts when anxious. This is likely to include different ways of avoiding or escaping from the frightening situation, but may also include other behaviors such as pacing, hitting, throwing tantrums, asking for help, or biting nails. Once again, the best idea is simply to ask children to think of the last few times they became worried or frightened and then get them to think of all the different things that they did.

Linking Thoughts and Feelings

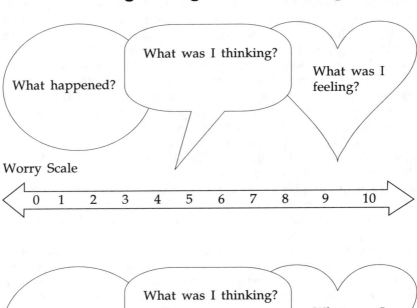

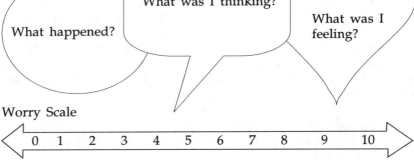

Figure 2.5   Linking Thoughts and Feelings

Practice Learning about Thoughts and Worries

As we said before, it's important for your child to learn to become more aware of his or her own patterns of anxiety. Since you're going to be helping your child through this program, it's a good idea for you to learn a little more about these patterns as well. You can do this by having your child keep a record of his or her anxiety for a week or two, until he or she can record a number of examples.

The form "linking thoughts and feelings," on the previous page, can be useful in tracking your child's progress. You'll want to make more copies of this page so you can use it throughout the program. Your child should make an entry on the sheet whenever he or she feels anxious, worried, shy, or scared, even if only a little. This may be many times a day, or only once a day. But you should try to encourage your child to make at least one entry each day. The sheet asks children to write the situation that made them frightened, their thoughts at the time, how they actually felt (e.g. frightened, worried, shy, nervous, etc.), and the degree of fear or worry (using the worry scale).

If your child is young (perhaps six to eight years), you'll likely need to be quite involved in helping to fill out this form. Older children may be relied on more to do it themselves, but you should still help to remind them. Your child should leave the worksheet somewhere that is easy to see so they remember to complete it every day. Remember that it's very important to praise and reward your child during the week for filling in the worksheet.

In Summary

- It'll be important to get your child motivated to tackle his or her anxiety before beginning the exercises.

- Most children find the program fun, and your praise, attention, and even some more tangible rewards can all help to encourage your child.

- Throughout the program you and your child will need to practice regularly and keep records of your practice.

- Your child will need to learn to rate his or her anxiety on a scale from 0–10.

- Your child should learn how anxiety influences the body, thoughts, and behaviors.

- In particular, your child needs to learn how specific thoughts are connected with specific feelings.

Chapter 3

Learning to Think Realistically

Chapter Objectives

By the time you've finished working through this chapter, you'll have a good understanding of:

- the relationship between events, thoughts, and feelings

- the importance of thoughts in producing your child's anxiety

- ways of helping your child to change his or her unrealistic thoughts by looking at evidence

Learning to think more realistically is a very useful strategy to help any person, adult or child, master anxiety. It will be particularly helpful as a part of your child's program. However, it is not an easy technique to use properly, even for adults. Therefore, in order to be able to really help your child use this skill, it is best if you can learn to use it yourself. For this reason, we have written this chapter in two parts. In the first part, we teach the ideas and methods of realistic thinking to you so that you can fully understand how it works. Because it is a complex technique, we recommend that you also use realistic thinking in your own life for a while to help you with any situations of worry, stress, or anger. Putting it into practice in this way will help you to better understand how it works. In the second part of the chapter, we show you how you can teach realistic thinking to your child. This is done in a way that is a simplified from the full technique that you will learn.

The Relationship Between Events, Thoughts, and Feelings

Most people think that events happening outside them cause feelings. In other words, if you experience a certain event, then certain feelings will be the inevitable result. For example, how many times have you said, "You made me so angry," or "That noise scared me"? However, outside events such as a traffic light or another person cannot be fully responsible for your feelings. One way to understand this is to realize that two people can experience exactly the same event, and feel very differently about it. Furthermore, the same person can experience the same event at different times and feel quite differently about it at each time. Why is this?

The answer lies in the content of your beliefs, thoughts, or self-talk—in other words, your feelings depend on what you are telling yourself about an event. As you will see in the following examples, it is your *beliefs* about a situation or event that determine how you will feel about that situation or event.

Imagine that both Tony's and Jim's wives are an hour late in coming home from the movies. Tony tells himself that his wife probably decided to have coffee with her friend (this is his belief about the situation). As a result of holding this belief, he is unconcerned about her, although somewhat annoyed that she didn't think to call and let him know. Jim, on the other hand, tells himself that his wife must have been involved in a car accident (this is his belief about the situation). As a direct result of holding this belief, he is worried sick.

This example clearly demonstrates that it is not the situation per se (wife being late) that results in the emotions experienced by each man. Instead, it's the beliefs or thoughts that are responsible for the different reactions. The event might act as a trigger, but the emotion that trigger produces depends on how the event is interpreted by the person. Let's look at another example, in which we can see different emotions experienced by the same individual, apparently in response to the same situation.

Celine has just finished a hard day's work and she is feeling tired and irritable. She gets home just as her husband, Aaron, is feeding their young son, Charles. When Aaron leaves for a few minutes, Charles begins playing with his food and, laughing, suddenly picks up the bowl and puts the whole meal on top of his head. He thinks this is hilarious, but Celine is furious at the mess. On another night, exactly the same thing happens. But this time, Celine has just been given a promotion at work and is feeling pretty good. This time, when Charles tips the bowl over his head, Celine thinks it's the cutest thing and laughs along. Here again, we can see an example of two different emotions being triggered by the same event, but this time it is happening in the same person. The difference lies entirely in what is going on inside Celine's head. In one case, Celine thinks about the mess and the inconvenience and becomes angry. In the other case, Celine thinks how cute her son is and how much fun he is having, and she feels good.

Although it's tempting to believe that an event itself determines the way in which we react to it, in actual fact, it's our beliefs and thoughts, based on our interpretations of that event, that directly determine how we react. As you help your child through this program, try to remind yourself and your child that our emotions are not directly caused by the things that go on around us. Instead, our feelings and emotions are the direct result of the way that we think about, or interpret, events and situations.

EVENT ⟶ BELIEF/THOUGHT ⟶ FEELING

Two Common Errors in Thinking

Most people who worry a lot or feel stressed tend to make two errors in their thinking. First, they commonly overestimate how likely it is that bad events will occur. Second, they usually assume that the outcomes or consequences of feared events will be catastrophic and unbearable.

Overestimating Probability

Someone who is an anxious person often believes that bad things are very likely to happen to them, even though this may not be true. Think, for example, of someone who is very shy having to get up and give a speech at a wedding. They may well think, "I just know that I'm going to say the wrong thing." Now, it is possible that they will end up saying something a little inappropriate. But it's quite hard to say the wrong thing at a wedding, and the chance that they will say the wrong thing is probably not very high. Thinking "I *am* going to say the wrong thing," implies 100 percent— that is, that you will definitely—say the wrong thing. Clearly, this is an overestimate.

Similarly, if you're late coming home, your child would feel anxious if she or he believes "Mom and Dad have had an accident." But this thought again implies 100 percent—Mom and Dad have *definitely* had an accident. While there may be some chance that you have had an accident, the reality is that it is probably pretty unlikely. So, your child thinking that it is definite is an overestimate that only serves to intensify anxiety.

Overestimating Consequences

To highly stressed people, life often seems very threatening. Not only do they believe that unpleasant things are highly likely to happen to them, they also believe that if those things do happen, the consequences will be absolutely catastrophic and intolerable.

Interestingly, most people who assume the worst are unaware they are doing it. In other words, they typically have never asked themselves the question, "What's the worst thing that could happen, and could I cope if it did happen?" For instance, imagine that you are on your way to an appointment. As you sit in your car, stuck in traffic, you think to yourself, "Oh no, I'm going to be really late." As part of this thought, you are assuming that being late will be really terrible. In other words, "I am going to be late, and that is the end of the world." But if you could ask yourself the question "If I am late, what will really happen and will I be able to cope with that?", you will probably find that being late is not really as tragic as you are assuming.

As another example, imagine that your child is very anxious about making a mistake on his or her homework. As part of this fear, she or he is probably assuming that making a mistake will be the "end of the world." In fact, while the teacher may make a comment about it, making a mistake in homework will probably have no serious effects at all. This shows you the second type of common problem in thinking: overestimating the consequences of things.

Changing Your Beliefs

So if our feelings come directly from our beliefs about a situation and anxious people tend to believe that bad things are more likely to happen to them than they really are, it seems reasonable that if we could change those beliefs, we could control our anxiety to some extent.

Before we go any further, we need to point out an important limitation. No one can ever control their thoughts and beliefs 100 percent, and so no one is going to be able to control their feelings 100 percent. That is not what we want to do. What we are aiming for is to teach you how to help your child control his or her extreme beliefs to a small degree. By doing this, children will also be able to reduce their extreme emotions to a small degree. This is one small step in learning to overcome anxiety.

The answer to reducing extreme anxiety is to learn how you might change your beliefs from extreme ones to less extreme ones. For example, instead of thinking, "My partner has been in a car accident, and he or she has been killed," you need to think, "There is a chance that my partner has been in a car accident, but it's more likely that there is another reason for his or her lateness. And even if she or he has had an accident, it's probably not a huge one." If you believed the second thought, your anxiety would be less.

The key to changing your emotions is belief. In other words, there is no point simply saying to yourself, "My partner hasn't been killed in a car accident," if you don't believe it. You have to convince yourself that the less extreme thought is true. Luckily, in most cases it is, and so it's usually not too hard to think of the less extreme thought. In most cases in life, the extreme, catastrophic belief is just not very realistic. Usually, the less extreme belief is the more realistic one. That is why we call this technique "realistic thinking" (note: when explaining it to your child, you might want to call it "detective thinking," which we will describe later in this chapter). Most people who are anxious tend to think in unrealistic ways. By learning to think more realistically, they can learn to control their anxiety.

Of course, an important point that this raises is that at times, things will happen in life that *are* bad. At these times, it's quite understandable and appropriate to be anxious. The goal, then, is not to try to teach your child never to be anxious. Rather, you can teach him or her a way of managing anxiety most of the time, when that anxiety is excessive and out of proportion to the real situation.

Looking at Evidence

The key to changing your thoughts is to really believe the new thoughts. That is, to convince yourself that your original belief is simply not true. We do this by learning to look at the actual evidence. In other words, you need to become a sort of detective or scientist with respect to your life and look at evidence for every negative thing that you believe. For kids we talk about "detective thinking," and later we will be showing you how you can teach your child to think like a detective.

To do detective thinking for yourself, this is what you need to do. Every time you find that you are stressed, anxious, or worried, you need to ask yourself, "What is the negative thing that I am expecting?" or "What do I think is going to go wrong here?" The answer to this question will give you your negative thought or belief. For example, imagine that you're walking down the street and you walk past a work colleague. You smile as you pass each other, but he doesn't smile back. You find yourself feeling resentful. So you could ask yourself, "Why am I feeling so upset—what is the negative thing that I am expecting?" Your answer might then be, "Obviously he doesn't like me." This is your negative belief.

Once you have identified your negative belief, you need to look at the evidence that either supports or doesn't support it. There are many types of evidence you can look at, and each thought will require slightly different evidence. However, there are four common types of evidence that we use most often:

1. *Past experience.* One of the easiest sources of evidence is to ask yourself how often you have been in a similar situation and how many of those times it has worked out badly. Remember to be very honest with yourself—don't just look at the bad times, but take into account every time you have been in a similar situation. For example, you might ask yourself, "How many times in the past has an acquaintance not smiled at me, and how many of those times has it turned out that he or she didn't like me?"

2. *General information.* You can also often get good evidence by looking at general information relating to a situation or event. This information may take the form of common sense, logic, general knowledge, or even official statistics or research. For example, you might ask yourself, "Do people always smile at everyone who smiles at them?" or "Does not smiling always mean that someone doesn't like me?"

3. *Alternative explanations.* A very useful strategy is to try to think about other possible reasons for the event. The negative interpretation that you had might be one explanation, but are there others? For example, you might realize that your colleague might not have smiled at you because he felt unwell or because he didn't see you, or because he didn't recognize you out of context. In this case, there are at least three good reasons why he may not have

smiled at you, in addition to the negative belief. Therefore, the negative belief is not definite, but is simply one out of four possible reasons.

4. *Role reversal.* Finally, a very good source of evidence for some situations, especially interpersonal ones, is to mentally turn the situation around. Pretend that you are the other person and they are you. Then ask yourself how you would feel or what you would think if the situation was reversed. For example, you might ask yourself, "If my colleague had smiled at me first and I didn't return the smile, would this be because I didn't like him?" Hopefully, this type of evidence will very quickly help you to realize that there are many possible reasons why someone may not smile at another, and it's very unlikely to be because of dislike.

Looking at all of the evidence in this way can help to convince you that your negative belief ("he doesn't like me") is just not very likely, or is at least not as likely as you originally assumed. But there is one further step to changing your beliefs.

As we said earlier, anxious people tend to overestimate both the likelihood of something bad happening and also how bad it will be. The evidence we've looked at so far should help to reduce the likelihood estimate. But what about the consequence? To examine this, you need to ask yourself one last question—"So what?" In other words, you need to ask yourself, "What would really happen if the bad thing that I am expecting actually did happen?" This question will help you to identify two possible types of answers. One possibility is that you will realize very quickly that the bad thing you were worrying about really isn't so bad. The other possibility is that you will come up with another negative belief and you will then need to look at the evidence for that.

For example, you might ask yourself, "So what if my colleague doesn't like me?" One possible answer might be, "I guess I don't really care." If you really believe this, then you should find your annoyance immediately dropping. On the other hand, you may come up with a negative consequence such as, "If my colleague doesn't like me, then it must mean that nobody in the office likes me." In this case, you have now identified another extreme thought, and you should go ahead and look at the evidence for this. For example, you might look at the logic of the statement (just because one person doesn't like you, does it have to follow that nobody likes you?) or at past experience (have you ever not been liked by someone and at those times, were there other people who still did like you?).

Learning to apply realistic thinking to one's life is not easy and takes a lot of practice. In reading this section, you may be thinking, "Why are these guys telling me all this? I'm not the one with the problem." This may be true, but the truth is that we can all use realistic thinking at times. We all have times when we get angry, anxious, or stressed when it really isn't necessary. At these times, learning to think more realistically can help to make a difference. But it will only work if you learn it well and really practice at times when you are not too emotional. More importantly, you need to learn to do realistic thinking for your child. The best chance your child has for learning to think more realistically is if you and your child's other caregivers can use realistic thinking. This will help your child learn by copying you, and you will be better able to help your child if you know what you are doing. For these reasons we strongly urge you to practice realistic thinking right along with your child.

Teaching Your Child about Realistic Thinking

The points we have been discussing are not necessarily easy ones to understand, and it is even harder to apply these principles to your own thoughts and beliefs. So you can be excused for wondering how you are going to teach these ideas to your child. In short, the answer is that you will teach your child a simplified version of these principles.

By the time you have worked through this chapter, your child should have a good understanding of several important points. These points are made in the exercises and sections that you will be working through with your child. However, it is also important that you emphasize and reemphasize these points whenever you can. The key points are:

1. Thoughts are the things we say to ourselves in our head.

2. Thoughts are important because they cause feelings and behaviors.

3. Thoughts can be either calm or worried.

4. Worried thoughts can often be changed by being a good detective and looking for evidence.

The material that you'll be working through with your child consists of three distinct but related stages, each of which builds upon the stage before. The first stage involves helping your child to understand what thoughts are, and to become skilled at identifying his or her own thoughts. The second stage involves helping your child learn about the importance of thoughts, and the third stage involves helping your child challenge worried thoughts by acting as a detective and examining the evidence. In the following sections we will include some instructions that you can use to explain the ideas to your child, as well as some exercises to help him or her understand the ideas better.

Why Are Thoughts Important?

At this point, you will need to explain the underlying idea of realistic thinking to your child just as we described it at the beginning of this chapter. Of course, depending on your child's age, this will most likely need to be a more simplified version than was described earlier. For this reason, following is a sample script that you can use to explain the ideas to your child.

Thoughts are important because they cause feelings and behaviors. Sometimes we have calm thoughts that make you feel good, and make you behave in ways that lead to good results for you. Other times we have worried thoughts that make you feel bad, and make you behave in ways that lead to bad results for you. See if you can tell whose thoughts are helpful and whose thoughts are unhelpful in this example:

Sam is at the movie theater with his family. Just before the movie starts, he sees a friend from his class on the other side of the room. Sam waves and calls out to the friend. The friend does not respond. Sam thinks to himself: "He must not have heard me. I'll go over to where he's sitting after the movie has finished and say hello." Sam feels fine. He sits quietly in his seat and enjoys the movie. When it has finished, he goes over to the side of the theater where his friend is sitting and says hello. His friend is pleased to see Sam and they make arrangements to meet up the next day to play.

Tim is at the movie theater with his family. Just before the movie starts, he sees a friend from his class on the other side of the room. Tim waves and calls out to the friend. The friend does not respond. Tim thinks to himself: "Oh no. He ignored me. He must hate me. Everyone saw that he ignored me. I can't believe what a loser I am." Tim feels embarrassed and miserable. He doesn't enjoy the movie at all because he's too busy worrying about what happened with the friend. When he sees the boy at school on Monday, Tim avoids him.

Whose thoughts do you think were helpful in this situation? Whose thoughts were unhelpful? Why?

This example shows that:

1. *People can have different thoughts in the same situation.*

2. *Your thoughts are really important because they cause feelings and behaviors.*

Thought Exercises

Below are two exercises that you can use to help your child better understand the idea that a person can think in different ways in the same situation and that these different thoughts will lead to different feelings and behaviors.

Ambiguous Situations

An ambiguous situation is one that doesn't have a clear cause or outcome. This is where people who are anxious really have difficulties. If there are two possible beliefs in a situation, the anxious person will usually hold the negative belief. There are a series of pictures on the next pages that could have more than one cause, a negative cause or a neutral or positive cause. Show each one to your child and ask him or her to come up with at least two possible thoughts that the person could be holding in each picture. Try to make sure that your child comes up with at least one negative thought and one positive or neutral thought. Then point out to your child how each thought would result in a different feeling.

Alternatives

This second exercise is very similar to the previous one. It simply adds the extra step of connecting different thoughts with feelings and behaviors.

Following are four ambiguous situations. Ask your child to try to come up with two different thoughts or interpretations for each—one worried thought and one calm thought. Then ask your child to say how he or she would feel and what he or she would do in the case of each of the thoughts. Use this exercise to illustrate for your child the difference between worried and calm thoughts, as well as

Self-talk 1:   Seeing a big dog in the street

Self-talk 2:   Mom is home late

Figure 3.1   Different Types of Thoughts

Self-talk 3:   Your teacher asks you to give a talk to the class

Self-talk 4:   Meeting other kids

Figure 3.1   Different Types of Thoughts   *(continued)*

the connection between each of these types of thoughts and feelings and behaviors.

Situation: You hear some strange noises outside at night.			
	Thoughts	Feelings	Behaviors
Worried			
Calm			
Situation: You haven't done your homework for school.			
	Thoughts	Feelings	Behaviors
Worried			
Calm			
Situation: You want to invite a new friend to your party.			
	Thoughts	Feelings	Behaviors
Worried			
Calm			

Initially, children often have difficulty distinguishing thoughts from feelings. They may also have trouble identifying their thoughts (don't be surprised if at first your child gives you the dreaded "I don't know" response to the question, "What were you thinking?").

The key really is practice. To begin with, you might need to help your child with suggestions and prompts. As they get better, you should give less and less guidance. You may need to repeat this exercise several times using different situations.

The Detective Approach

As we discussed earlier, one of the most common mistakes that anxious, stressed children make in their thinking is to overestimate the probability that their negative, anxious interpretation of a situation is in fact true. For this reason, anxious children need to learn how to realistically evaluate the likelihood that their negative, anxious interpretations of situations are true or accurate. This will help them to really believe their helpful thoughts. Imagine that a child who experiences social anxiety believes, "If I ask the teacher a question in class, everyone will think I'm stupid." Imagine that the child is assigning a 100 percent probability value to this interpretation or belief—he or she believes it is definitely true. If this probability value could be reduced, the child would feel less anxious. This is the aim of the detective approach.

This approach involves children gathering together all the available evidence regarding a negative, unhelpful, or worried thought and then, on the basis of this evidence, realistically evaluating the likelihood that the anxious interpretation is accurate. When successful, this evaluation results in the assignment of a new, more realistic probability to the interpretation and a reduction in anxiety. Reducing the expected probability value assigned to negative, anxious interpretations is a gradual process that requires practice. It's essential that children truly believe in the lowered probability value. For this reason, it's important that you don't simply tell children that a certain interpretation is silly or unlikely, as they probably won't believe you. Instead, they need to come to the realization that their interpretation is unlikely themselves, through the process of gathering and evaluating the evidence.

In this approach, what children are being asked to do (gather evidence and, in light of this, evaluate their worried thoughts or interpretations) is very similar to the work done by detectives. Both are searching for evidence and clues in order to reach the "truth." It can be useful (particularly with younger children) to incorporate a favorite detective or superhero (such as Inspector Gadget, Wonder Woman, or Superman) into the detective approach, so that this character is helping the children search for clues and examine evidence. Once children get used to thinking about their favorite detective in this way, you can use this character as a prompt. In other words, when children begin to worry, you simply need to remind them to try to think like their detective.

This approach essentially involves three steps. The first step is for children to work out what they are worried about. They need to identify their worried thought. Remember to remind your child of the difference between thoughts and feelings. It's best if the worried thought is a clear statement of what your child expects to happen. For example, a thought such as "I'm scared that Dad has been killed in a car accident," is a good, clear description that your child can use with his or her detective thinking. In contrast, a thought such as "I'm scared because dad isn't here," doesn't say what your child is really afraid of and cannot be worked on easily.

The second step is for your child to gather as much evidence as possible about the worried thought. This is where children get to play detective and try to work out how they might really "know" whether the thing they're afraid of will really happen. The best types of evidence are listed:

- What has happened before in this situation?

- What general things do I know about this situation?

- What else could happen in this situation?

Finally, based on the evidence children have thought of, they'll be in a position to reevaluate the worried thought. Hopefully, they'll be able to realize that the worried thought isn't actually very likely and that a calm thought is more likely. Remember, this exercise is about *realistic* thinking, not positive thinking. This means that there will be some occasions when the worried thought is actually the more likely one. As an example, think of the child who goes out after dark and finds him or herself in a dark lane and sees someone breaking into a house. It is important to point out to children that in such situations feeling frightened is very natural and useful. The detective thinking that you're teaching your child is designed to help replace worried thoughts with calm thoughts at those times when your child's fears are excessive and unrealistic, not in all situations.

The Case of the Big Dog

Teaching your child to use detective thinking is probably best demonstrated with an example. This example shows Kurt, who was introduced to you in the first chapter, talking with his mother about one of Kurt's smaller fears—dogs. You'll need to go through lots of practices like this with your child over several weeks to help your child really learn how to use the detective approach. (An example of Kurt's detective thinking form appears on page 52, and blank forms for you to copy are on page 55.)

Mother: I want you to imagine that you're walking down the street one day when a big dog comes running up to you (write "A dog comes running up to me," on the *Event* line of the detective thinking form). If you were scared of the dog, what might you think to yourself, Kurt?

Kurt: If he was a really big dog, I would be scared that he was going to bite me.

Mother: Well done, Kurt! You've just worked out your worried thought. Let's write that down here (write "The dog is going to bite me" on the *What am I worried about* line). Now let's pretend that we're detectives and look at the evidence for whether this will or will not happen. What sort of evidence can you think of?

Kurt: You could run away from the dog.

Mother: Sure, that's one thing you could *do* in that situation. Can you think of any evidence for how you know whether the dog will bite you? For example, what has happened before when a dog came running up to you?

Kurt: I was at my Auntie's house once, and their big black dog Jack came running up to me.

Mother: What happened when it ran up to you?

Kurt: Nothing, it was friendly.

Mother: Good work. So a dog has run up to you before at your Auntie's house, and nothing bad happened. That sounds like an excellent bit of evidence to me. Let's write that down (write "A dog has come up to me before and it didn't bite me" on the *Evidence* line). What did you do when it came over?

Kurt: Well, I patted it. Its fur was really dirty.

Mother: Wow, you were so brave that you even patted it. That's fantastic. So, rather than the dog biting you, what could be the other possibility?

Kurt: It could be friendly, and I could pat it.

Mother: That's right. Rather than the dog wanting to bite you, the alternative possibility is that it's friendly and wants you to pat it. Do you think this could be a good piece of evidence?

Kurt: Yes.

Mother: Yes, I think so too. Good detective work. Let's put the alternative possibility in the *Evidence* line (write "The dog is being friendly and wants me to pat him," in the *Evidence* line). I have one more question for you: Are all dogs mean, or are lots quite friendly?

Kurt: Lots are quite friendly.

Mother: Okay, that's another useful piece of evidence (write "Lots of dogs are friendly," in the *Evidence* line). Now that we've looked at some evidence, do you really think that the dog is going to bite you?

Kurt: Probably not.

Mother: Good work. From the evidence we came up with it's probably more likely that it's friendly, and that nothing bad will happen. That sounds like a calm thought to me— let's write it here (write "The dog is probably friendly and nothing bad will happen," on the last line).

Mother: I'm wondering, how would you be feeling if you were thinking that the dog was going to bite you?

Kurt: Scared.

Mother: And, how would you be feeling if you were thinking that the dog was friendly?

Kurt: Good.

Mother: Excellent. You're very clever. We can see that the worried thought about the dog would make you feel scared, and this other calm thought would make you feel more happy and relaxed around the dog.

Explaining Detective Thinking to Your Child

In this next section we list some possible instructions you could use to help you to explain detective thinking to your child. It's the exceptional child (and parent) who understands the ideas and can use detective thinking right away. You'll need to be patient and keep reminding your child of the concepts and make sure he or she does lots and lots of practice. Practice will also be useful for you, since we find many parents who have quite a bit of difficulty with this skill. It's not shameful to admit you're having difficulty—don't be afraid to reread the sections and keep practicing.

Okay. You know now that some thoughts are unhelpful. They make you feel worried and scared; and they can make you do things that lead to bad results for you. Luckily, there are things you can do to beat the worried thoughts.

The first step is to catch them. You've already had some practice at this. Whenever you notice that you're feeling worried or scared or nervous, what you need to do is to catch the worried thought that's causing you to feel this way. Then, write it down on the detective thinking form, next to the "What am I worried about?" heading.

Kurt's Detective thinking

Event   *A dog comes running up to me.*

What am I worried about?	*The dog is going to bite me.*
What is the evidence? What happened when I was worried before? What are the facts? What else could happen?	*A dog has come up to me before, and it didn't bite me.* *The dog is being friendly and wants me to pat him.* *Lots of dogs are friendly.*
What is my calm thought? What will really happen?	*The dog is probably friendly and nothing bad will happen.*

The next step is to become a detective and hunt down all the evidence to do with the worried thought. A detective's job is to look for evidence and clues so that he or she can find out the truth. This is exactly what you need to do. Once you've identified the worried thought, you need to look at all the evidence and decide whether or not this worried thought is true. Here are some questions you can ask yourself to make sure that you consider all the evidence:

- *What has happened before in this situation? Have you been in a situation like this before? Did anything bad happen? Does something bad happen* every *time you're in the situation?*

- *What general background information do you know about this situation? Is it really a bad situation? Have any of your friends or people you know had anything like this happen to them?*

- *What else could happen in this situation? Is there another explanation?*

    Once you've collected your evidence, the last thing you need to do is to take it all into account and work out how much you believe in your worried thought (based on the evidence). The question to ask yourself here is, "Based on the evidence, what do I really think will happen? Can I think of a different, calm thought?" Write your calm thought on the last line of the detective thinking form.

Practicing Detective Thinking

Detective thinking probably won't be an easy skill for your child to learn. The key is practice. Make lots of copies of the blank detective thinking form for your child. Then tell children that they should fill in a section on the form every time they feel at all nervous, shy, worried, or frightened. It may be a good habit to sit down together each afternoon or evening, think through the day, and go over detective thinking for any bad experiences that day. Even doing them after the fact is good practice. The better children get, the more likely they'll be to begin to use detective thinking when they're actually feeling anxious. To begin, you'll probably need to be quite involved and help your child considerably. As he or she gets better, you should help less and less. Older children might pick up the skills in a few days, while younger children may need help for some time. But remember, this isn't a race—each child needs to take whatever time is needed to master the skill.

Obviously, the key is for your child to be able to use detective thinking when he or she is in a frightening situation. Therefore, whenever you notice your child getting nervous, try to prompt him or her to use this skill. Earlier on, you will need to prompt in detail, helping your child with the exact steps and questions. As he or she gets better at the skill, prompts may simply take the form of reminders such as "What would (his or her detective) think?" or "Why not try your detective thinking?"

Most importantly, you shouldn't be too perfectionistic or allow your child to be so regarding these skills. The goal is for your child to learn to replace worried thoughts with calm ones. Exactly how she or he gets to this point is not so important and may vary slightly from child to child. Some children, especially very young ones, may not be able to do the exact evidence collecting that we've suggested here. But they may still begin to think more calmly with practice. Remember also that this isn't the only technique for overcoming anxiety. So, if your child really cannot master detective thinking (after a good and serious try), you might want to move on and rely more on skills such as relaxation.

Summary

- Different people can have different thoughts in the same situation.

- The same person can have different thoughts in a given situation.

- Therefore, it's not the situation itself that causes our feelings. Rather, our feelings come directly from our thoughts, beliefs, and interpretations about a situation.

- Anxious children tend to have many worried thoughts, and these worried thoughts lead to feelings of fear and anxiety.

- Using the detective approach, anxious children can be taught to challenge their worried thoughts and work out whether they're really true.

- Detective thinking involves: identifying the worried thought; examining evidence for that thought (such as previous experience, other explanations, and logic) and looking for a more likely calm thought.

Detective thinking

Event

What am I worried about?	
What is the evidence? What happened when I was worried before? What are the facts? What else could happen?	
What is my calm thought? What will really happen?	

Event

What am I worried about?	
What is the evidence? What happened when I was worried before? What are the facts? What else could happen?	
What is my calm thought? What will really happen?	

Chapter 4

How Can Your Child Learn to Relax?

Objectives

In this chapter you will learn:

- to understand the importance of relaxation
- to teach your child how to identify feelings of muscle tension and relaxation
- to help your child to relax the whole body
- to teach your child to relax deeply using breathing and imagery methods
- to teach your child to use relaxation to cope with stressful situations

Relaxation Can Alleviate Anxiety

All children experience physical and emotional tension in response to stressful events at some time in their lives. Very high levels of negative emotions such as anxiety, anger, guilt, or fear will make it difficult for children to use the coping skills that you're trying to teach them. For this reason, it may be important to teach children how to reduce these negative emotions to a level that allows them to use their coping skills.

One strategy that children can use to cope with stress and to keep anxiety under control is relaxation. During relaxation, our thoughts become calm and peaceful, blocking out anxious and worrying issues. Our body reactions change so that our heartbeat slows down and our muscle tension decreases. Signs of muscle tightness gradually disappear. These reductions in body tension and worrisome thoughts produce an emotional feeling of calmness and well-being. It's difficult to feel really anxious at the same time as feeling really relaxed. If children can learn to reduce the physical and emotional reactions to stress through the use of relaxation methods, then they'll be more able to apply their coping skills.

Some of the different ways that children can learn how to relax include listening to relaxing, peaceful music; meditation; relaxing imagery; muscle relaxation exercises; deep breathing exercises; yoga; and massage. We're going to describe one particular method of relaxation that many children and their parents find effective. One of the best ways to teach children how to relax is to have the whole family involved in practicing and using the relaxation exercises. The method that is presented here combines a variety of techniques, and you may want to adapt the exercises to suit you and your family.

Teaching Your Child to Relax

Before you start to teach your child how to relax, there are a few points that we need to discuss and that will help you in these teaching sessions.

Relaxation Is a Skill

Like all new skills, relaxation exercises have to be practiced regularly in order to be performed well. You and your child will need to practice every day. To encourage you to practice regularly, we ask you to keep a record of your practice sessions on the relaxation record form provided.

Teaching your child to relax also involves starting at the beginning, teaching the simple steps first. Then, when these can be performed well, you can move on to teaching more complex relaxation skills. It will probably take at least a week of daily practice in order for your child to relax well. After that, it's important to keep up daily practice while you go through the other steps in this book. Relaxation will be a useful technique for children to use when they're trying out some of their anxiety management skills later on.

It's important to fill in the relaxation monitoring form every time you practice (every day). Following is a copy and you should make many copies of the blank form for your child to use. It's a good idea to keep the relaxation monitoring form in a clearly visible place where you're likely to see it each day (such as on the fridge). This will help to remind you to do the relaxation practice.

Relaxation Record Form

Please fill in this record form each day. Put a circle around the answer.

	Did you do relaxation practice?	How long?	How relaxed did your child become?		
Monday	Yes No		Not at all	A bit	Very
Tuesday	Yes No		Not at all	A bit	Very
Wednesday	Yes No		Not at all	A bit	Very
Thursday	Yes No		Not at all	A bit	Very
Friday	Yes No		Not at all	A bit	Very
Saturday	Yes No		Not at all	A bit	Very
Sunday	Yes No		Not at all	A bit	Very

Note: Older children can fill in this form themselves.

Pick the Right Time

There are several things that you can do to make learning to relax an enjoyable activity. It's important to pick the right time to practice. We suggest that you pick a time when there are no other important things to do. For example, don't pick a time when your child's favorite TV show is on. Many families decide to get up ten to fifteen minutes earlier each day to do their relaxation practice. Others may set aside time before their child goes to bed. Before bed is often a convenient time, but you need to make sure that your child isn't too tired to concentrate on learning the skills. Using relaxation as a way to get to sleep is fine, but practicing relaxation needs to be done at a time when your child can concentrate.

Making the Time

It's easy to allow relaxation practice to be pushed out by other activities such as homework, sports, TV, and just general living. Setting aside a regular time for relaxation benefits the whole family. It makes everyone in the family aware that life can easily be taken over by rushing around and not taking time to look after our emotional well-being.

Creating a Habit

One of the best ways of making sure that relaxation practice takes place is to set up a daily habit. Gradually, relaxation will become an automatic activity that's built into the family routine. In the same way that cleaning our teeth becomes an automatic response every day, relaxation practice can become one of our daily habits. Try not to start missing days, and have a stand-by time that can be used if your regular practice time is not possible.

Creating a Relaxing Environment

When your child is learning to relax, you need to create an environment that will encourage relaxation. The area needs to be quiet, where you will not be disturbed. You may want to take the phone off the hook or put on the answering machine. If you're thinking of inviting visitors over, make sure that it doesn't conflict with relaxation practice. The place of practice needs to be warm and comfortable. You can use a bed, a comfortable chair, or a mat on the floor. But if you use a bed, make sure you and your child don't fall asleep. Relaxation practice is easier if you and your child are wearing comfortable, casual clothes. Some families like to put on some quiet, calming music. Children respond well to relaxing music and it may be useful to set the scene for practice by putting this type of music on in the background.

Use Praise and Make It Fun

As with all the methods in this book, you'll need to use plenty of praise to encourage your child to practice and use the skills. Remember to give praise for trying, not just for succeeding in relaxation. As much as possible, try to make relaxation time an enjoyable, fun experience. There are plenty of ways to make relaxation practice interesting. In some of the steps you'll be using imagery, where children imagine themselves in peaceful, relaxing situations. You can use wonderful examples here of situations that children will love, such as magical islands, secret gardens, sailing ships, and so on. These will all help to make the sessions interesting and enjoyable.

Keep It Simple and Short

Children tend to lose interest quickly and find it hard to pay attention for long periods. With young children, it's better to practice more often for shorter periods, such as five minutes. You also need to use simple language so that your child can understand the instructions.

Teaching by Example

In the following section of this chapter, you will find a series of steps for learning relaxation skills. Depending on the age of your child, you'll probably need to be the teacher of these skills. Some older children and adolescents find it difficult to accept instructions and guidance from their parents and prefer to read through the book and practice the skills on their own. However, one of the best ways to teach young children how to relax is to show them how to perform each step. This involves actually demonstrating each step by doing it yourself. It's really important with each step that you explain out loud exactly what you are doing and why you are doing it. That way, children gradually learn to say these instructions to themselves quietly and can eventually instruct themselves to use the relaxation methods.

The Final Goal

The goal is for children to be able to use their relaxation skills to relax when they become afraid and when they try to face difficult situations. However, it's important that the skills are learned really well at home first. Also, daily relaxation as a habit for the whole family creates a general atmosphere of calmness at home that benefits everybody.

Steps to Relaxation

Step 1: Learning to Tense and Relax the Muscles

One of the best places to start is to learn the difference between being tense and being relaxed. Following are the instructions for how to do this. The words in italics show the sorts of instructions that you should say aloud to your child. You need to perform the actions too, as you give the instructions.

> *First, take your right arm and push it out in front of you. I want you to feel what it's like when your muscles are really tense and tight. Try to imagine that you have a tennis ball in your hand and you're trying to squeeze it really hard. Now really clench your fist and squeeze as tightly as you can. Count slowly to five while you hold it tight ... one ... two ... three ... four ... five.... Can you tell me how your hand feels when it's all tensed up? What do your muscles feel like?*

(Encourage your child to come up with words like tight, stiff, gripping.)

> *Now try again. Really clench your fist and squeeze as tightly as you can. Count slowly to five while you hold it tight ... one ... two ... three ... four ... five.... Now let go. Let your hand and fingers go limp and loose. Let them go all floppy, so that your hand drops back by your side. Can you describe to me how your hand feels when it's relaxed?*

(Encourage your child to come up with words such as droopy, loose, floppy, or other words that children would use to describe a relaxed state.)

> *Good, so you can see the difference in your muscles when they're tense compared to when they're relaxed. What we're going to do in this exercise is learn to relax the muscles in our bodies so that we can relax at times when we get all tensed up. There are lots of times when we get tensed up, like when we are frightened, nervous, worried, or angry. Relaxing helps you to feel better in difficult times. Learning to relax is just like learning to ride your*

bike or roller-skate or anything else. You have to practice, and bit by bit you'll find that it gets easier to do. Now we're going to relax the arms even more deeply.

While you're giving the following instructions, try to keep your voice calm and peaceful, speaking rather slowly. When you say words like "relax," "calm," or "deeper," make your voice sound really relaxed.

Push both of your arms out in front of you and keep them still and straight. Now push your arms down into your chair (or the floor) and try to push your body upward, so that your arms are really tight. Now take a deep breath and hold your arms tight, clench your fists too, while you count to one ... two ... three ... four ... five. Now, let it go. Breathe out and let your arms relax. Make sure that you keep your eyes closed. Let your arms drop down by your sides, until they just hang there. Limp and loose like a rag doll. Or you could imagine that you're a jellyfish, just a large lump of floppy jelly. Now, concentrate on relaxing the muscles in your arms. Try to feel what the muscles in your arms feel like and let them go limp. Check your right arm first and let it go very floppy. Now move your attention to your left arm, and let it become heavy and droopy. Relax. Can you feel any tightness? If you can, then try to let your arms go even floppier. Your arms are really starting to relax now. Really relaxed, really relaxed. Further and further, deeper and deeper, more and more relaxed. Let both arms relax together now. Relax.

(Relax quietly for a minute.)

Relax. Really relax.

(Relax quietly for another minute.)

Good, now in a moment, I'm going to ask you to slowly open your eyes. I'll count to ten, and when I get to five, I'd like you to open your eyes. Then, when I get to ten, I will ask you to slowly sit up. One ... two ... three ... four ... five. Now, slowly open your eyes ... six ... seven ... eight ... nine ... ten. Now slowly sit up and have a stretch. How did that feel? How relaxed did you become?

Tensing and relaxing the arms should be repeated two or three times in the session. You can check if your child is relaxing well. When you lift your child's arm up, it should drop back gently when you let go. We suggest that you and your child practice step 1 at least twice before moving on to step 2.

Step 2: Relaxing the Rest of the Body

Once your child is able to relax his or her arms really well, then you can move on to tense and relax the rest of the body. Begin by relaxing the arms, first, as described above. Then, with the arms relaxed, you can move on to other muscle groups. Remember to use a calm, relaxed, and gentle voice while you're giving the instructions.

> *Now let's move on to the muscles in your head and face. Try to screw up your face so that it looks awful. Screw up your eyes, your lips, even your tongue in your mouth. Now take a deep breath and hold while I count to five . . . one . . . two . . . three . . . four . . . five. Now, let it go. Breathe out and let your face relax. Make sure that you keep your eyes closed. Now, concentrate on relaxing the muscles in your face. Feel what your forehead feels like and let it go all limp. Now move your attention to your eyes, and let them become heavy and droopy. Relax your mouth and lips. Try to feel what your lips feel like. Can you feel any tightness? If you can, then try to let them go all floppy. Even your tongue should be relaxed, so try and think about what your tongue feels like and relax it. You can relax your whole face and head now, really relax. Your head might even feel as though it's too heavy for your neck. Further and further, deeper and deeper, more and more relaxed. Let the whole of your face relax together. Relax.*

(Relax for a minute.)

> *Now we're going to tense and relax the lower part of our bodies. This includes our backs, tummies, and legs. This time I want you to imagine that you're a stiff robot. Pull in the muscles in your tummy. Good. Now lift your legs up in the air, keeping them straight and screw up your toes. Really make them stiff, just like that metal robot. Now take a deep breath and hold it while I count to five, and keep your legs and tummy tight. . . . one . . . two . . . three . . . four . . . five. Now, let yourself relax. Breathe out through your mouth. Concentrate on relaxing the muscles in your tummy. There shouldn't be any tightness in your stomach muscles now. Let the muscles go all floppy. Feel what your back feels like too, and let it go all limp. Now move your attention to your legs, and let them become heavy and droopy. Relax the top part of your legs and gradually move down your legs, relaxing*

each muscle in turn. Relax your knees, your calves, your ankles and now your feet and toes. Just try to imagine that any tightness and tension is moving down your body, down and down, down through your legs, and out through your toes. Imagine that the tightness is drifting out into the air, leaving your body feeling really relaxed. So relaxed that you almost feel like a rag doll. Imagine that I come over and pick you up and shake you gently. Your legs and arms are all floppy when I pick you up. There's no tightness in your neck, so your head just drops forward. Your arms and legs just hang there at your sides. Really relax. Further and further, deeper and deeper, more and more relaxed. Let all your muscles relax together. Relax.

(Relax for a minute.)

Relax . . . relax . . . relax. Good, now in a moment, I'm going to ask you to slowly open your eyes. I will count to ten, and when I get to five, I'd like you to open your eyes. Then, when I get to ten, I will ask you to slowly sit up. One . . . two . . . three . . . four . . . five. Now slowly open your eyes . . . six . . . seven . . . eight . . . nine . . . ten. How did that feel? How relaxed did you become?

It's important to practice going through the different muscle groups, tensing and relaxing them until your child is really good at relaxing all the parts of the body. This step should be practiced every day for two or three days, or until he or she is able to relax really well. Each time, starting with the arms, then the head and face, moving on to the legs, and finishing with the torso (stomach, bottom, chest, and back). Immediately after the relaxation, you might ask your child to color in the following picture to show which parts of the body felt the most relaxed. This will help you identify any parts of the body that your child finds hard to relax, and then you can spend some extra time on relaxing this area in the next practice session. Although you're aiming for your child to feel really relaxed, this relaxation does not need to be "perfect."

Step 3: Relaxing the Whole Body at Once

Once your child is able to relax each of their body parts in turn, you can move on to relaxing the whole body at once. All children are different in the speed with which they learn relaxation skills. The speed of learning also depends upon how often you both practice

Color in this picture to show how relaxed the parts of your body are.

Color red if the body part was very tense and tight.
Color yellow if the body part was a bit relaxed.
Color blue if the body part was really relaxed.

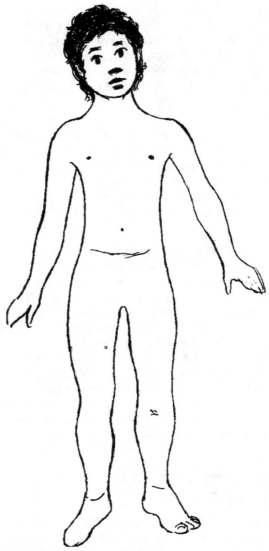

Figure 4.1   Relaxation Successes

the skills. Some children are ready to move on to stage 3 after just a couple of days of practicing stage 2. Other children may need to work on stage 2 every day for two to three weeks before they're able to relax each part of the body really well. We suggest that you and your child decide together when to move on to the next step. It's important not to spend too many days on each stage, as your child may become bored.

Following are the instructions for step 3:

Now let's try to tighten up your whole body at once. Watch me first. I take a deep breath ... screw up my face ... push up my shoulders into my neck ... arms pushing down against the chair, stomach pulled in ... and legs lifted upwards ... even my fists are clenched and my toes are screwed up. I hold this while I count to five, and then I let go: one ... two ... three ... four ... five, and breathe out and relax.

Now you try. Tense up first. Take a deep breath ... screw up your face ... push up your shoulders into your neck ... push your arms down against the chair, tummy pulled in ... and legs lifted upwards ... clench your fists and screw up your toes. Make your body go stiff all over. Imagine that you're a robot. Hold it there while you count to five: one ... two ... three ... four ... five, and now breathe out. Let yourself go all floppy and limp. Imagine that you're a rag doll who doesn't have any bones or stiffness in your body. Let yourself go absolutely limp and loose all over. Let your breathing become gentle now. Just concentrate on letting your body relax. Really relax. Close your eyes and try to concentrate on what we're doing. Try not to let other thoughts wander into your head.

Breathe out and let your arms relax. Concentrate on relaxing the muscles in your arms. Let your arms flop down by your sides, until they just hang there. Limp and loose like that rag doll or that jelly fish. Try to feel what the muscles in your arms feel like and let them go all limp. Check your right arm first and let it go completely limp. Now think about your other arm, and let it become heavy and droopy too. Relax. Can you feel any tightness? If you can, then try to let your arms go even floppier. Your arms are really starting to relax now. Really relaxed, really relaxed. Further and further, deeper and deeper, more and more relaxed. Let both arms relax together now. Relax.

Now let's move on to the muscles in your head and face. Breathe out and let your face relax. Make sure that you keep your eyes closed. Now, concentrate on relaxing the muscles in your face. Feel what your forehead feels like and let it go all limp.

Now move your attention to your eyes and let them become heavy and droopy. Relax your mouth and lips. Try to focus on what your lips feel like. Can you feel any tightness? If you can, then try to let them go all floppy. Even your tongue should be relaxed, so try and focus on what your tongue feels like and relax it. You can relax your whole face and head now, really relax. Further and further, deeper and deeper, more and more relaxed. Let the whole of your face relax. Really relax.

Now move your attention to your legs and let them become heavy and floppy. Relax the top part of your legs and gradually move down your legs, relaxing each muscle in turn. Relax your knees, your calves, your ankles, and now your feet and toes. Just try to imagine that any tightness and tension is moving down your body, down and down, down through your legs, and out through your toes. Imagine the tightness is drifting out into the air, leaving your body and legs feeling really relaxed. So relaxed that you can almost feel like that rag doll. Imagine that I come over and pick you up and gently shake you. Your legs and arms are all floppy, and they shake when I pick you up. There is no tightness in your neck so your head just drops forward. Your arms and legs just hang there at your sides. Really relax. Further and further, deeper and deeper, more and more relaxed.

Now, think about the muscles in your tummy. There shouldn't be any tightness in your stomach muscles now. Let the muscles go all floppy. Feel what your back feels like too, and let it go all limp. Relax. Now, I want you to let your muscles relax a little bit more and a little bit more. Last of all, think about relaxing your chest. Can you feel your chest? Really relax the muscles of your chest as you breathe out, really deeply relaxing.

Go back to the top of your head and work downward, checking each muscle that you come to. Check if it feels at all tense or tight. Then say to yourself "relax" and let all the tightness drift away. Really relax now. Starting at the top of your head, relax. Moving down . . . through your arms and chest . . . and down . . . past your back and your tummy, and down through your legs. Muscle by muscle, really relaxing. Relax . . . relax . . . relax.

Let all your muscles go limp and loose. Imagine waves of tightness leaving your body through your fingers and toes. Drifting out into the air, leaving your arms and legs feeling really relaxed and loose. Down now through your legs, past your knees and calves, through your ankles, and out through your toes. Let all the tightness leave your body now. Leaving you really relaxed. Further and further, deeper and deeper, more and more relaxed. Imagine that you're that rag doll. All limp and loose and floppy. If anyone picked you up, your arms and legs would hang by your sides. There is no tightness anywhere in your body.

Good, now in a moment, I'm going to ask you to slowly open your eyes. I'll count to ten, and when I get to five, I'd like you to open your eyes. Then, when I get to ten, I'll ask you to slowly sit up. One ... two ... three ... four ... five. Now slowly open your eyes ... six ... seven ... eight ... nine ... ten. Now slowly sit up. Try not to put all the tension straight back into your muscles. Try to stay relaxed. Good. How did you feel? How relaxed did you become?

By now you and your child (and family if everyone is taking part) will be getting good at relaxing quickly and deeply. This step usually needs to be practiced every day for at least two to three days or more. Remember that learning to relax is like learning to ride a bike. The more you practice, the easier it will be.

Step 4: Using Breathing and Imagery to Relax Further

Once your child has mastered relaxation of the whole body, then it's time to learn to relax even more deeply. There are several ways to increase the depth of relaxation. One method is to use breathing techniques. The aim is to focus attention on breathing in a relaxed way. Make sure that your child doesn't try to breathe too quickly, deeply, or shallowly or they may feel dizzy. The aim is to produce even, gentle, and relaxed breathing.

Relaxing images or pictures in the mind are also a useful way to relax even more deeply. Our imagination can be used to help us feel really relaxed. Children have really good imaginations and are able to relax beautifully with the help of imagery. When you give instructions for imagery, there are certain things that help. You'll need to describe scenes in a way that helps your child conjure up the image. You need to describe exactly what can be seen in the picture: the shapes, colors, and textures, and the sounds that can be heard, the smells that are there, and any sensations from touch. The description of senses helps to create a vivid image. Remember also to select imagery scenes that will appeal to children and that are relaxing in content. The scenes shouldn't be too lively or exciting. The aim is to pick scenes that are likely to produce feelings of deep relaxation, calmness, safety, and peace. Following is one example of this technique. Begin with whole body relaxation and breathing techniques. Move on to the imagery once your child is reasonably relaxed.

The session should begin by relaxing all the muscles of the body first as described in step 3. After tensing the whole body and then relaxing each muscle group in turn:

> *Concentrate on the feelings of the air moving into your lungs and out again. Try to breathe in through your nose and out through your mouth. Concentrate hard on this until you can feel the air moving in through your nose, into your lungs, and then back out through your mouth. The air may feel cool and light. Feel the air moving across your lips on its way out. Now, keep your eyes closed and try to imagine that you're holding a candle just in front of you, a few inches from your face, but not close enough for it to feel hot. Imagine that as you breathe out, the air moves across your lips and makes the candle flame flicker. Really concentrate on imagining that this is really happening, until you can imagine that the candle is really there and flickering. Good, stay relaxed, and with every breath now I want you to relax a little bit deeper each time you breathe out. Breathe in . . . and out . . . in . . . and out.*

(Try to time this to even, gentle breathing.)

> *Each time you breathe out, say to yourself "relax . . . relax." Imagine that the candle flickers each time you breathe out as you relax further and further, deeper and deeper, getting more and more relaxed. Let your breathing stay even and gentle, not too fast or deep. Really gentle and calm. Relax . . . relax.*
>
> *Good. Now in a moment, I'm going to ask you to slowly open your eyes. I'll count to ten, and when I get to five, I would like you to open your eyes. Then, when I get to ten, I will ask you to slowly sit up. One . . . two . . . three . . . four . . . five. Slowly open your eyes, six . . . seven . . . eight . . . nine . . . ten.*
>
> *Now slowly sit up. Try not to put all the tension straight back into your muscles. Try to stay relaxed. How did you feel?*
>
> *Now you're going to use your imagination to relax even more deeply. Close your eyes and try to listen to what I'm saying. Try not to let your thoughts drift off onto other things. Imagine now that you're lying on the beach. You have plenty of sunscreen on and it's a warm sunny day. The beach is very quiet. You've had a swim and you're feeling rather tired, so you lie down on your towel. Your friends are having a quiet time too and nobody disturbs you. You lie in the sun and let your body*

relax. Really relax. You can feel the warmth of the sand through your towel and your body begins to feel warm and peaceful. You can see the sky—it's clear and blue with tiny white fluffy clouds. The sea looks clear and blue and sparkles in the sun. You can see a bird flying way up in the sky. Watch the bird as it floats in the wind. Now concentrate on what you can hear. You can hear the sound of the surf gently rolling against the beach. What else can you hear? What else can you see? Now think about what you can feel with your fingers. You reach out and run your fingers through the sand. It feels warm and the grains of sand run through your fingers. Just imagine that you lie there relaxing, with your muscles becoming more and more relaxed. There's nothing to disturb you. You feel calm and peaceful. No worries, no problems. Just really relaxed and calm. Further and further, deeper and deeper, more and more relaxed.

Now, I want you to spend just a couple of minutes letting your muscles relax a little bit more and a little bit more. Try to keep that scene of being at the beach in your imagination. Just let the whole of your body relax ... really deeply ... further and further, deeper and deeper ... relax ... relax ... relax.

Good. Now in a moment, I'm going to ask you to slowly open your eyes. I'll count to ten, and when I get to five, I'd like you to open your eyes. Then, when I get to ten, I'll ask you to slowly sit up. One ... two ... three ... four ... five. Slowly open your eyes ... six ... seven ... eight ... nine ... ten.

Now slowly sit up. Try not to let all the tension straight back into your muscles. Try to stay relaxed. Good. How did you feel? Were you able to imagine being on the beach? Could you imagine the feelings of the sand and the warm sun? How relaxed did you become?

More Imagery Scenes

There are many other imagery scenes that can be used to help children relax. Each session should begin with tension of the whole body and then relaxation of each muscle starting from the head and working downward. Instructions are then given to concentrate on relaxed breathing, prior to the introduction of a relaxing imagery scene. Here are some ideas that you might like to use to develop some more imagery scripts with your child:

- lying by the pool at a friend's house

- lying on a picnic blanket and talking to a good friend

- sitting on the veranda at Grandma's
- watching the sunset
- floating in space
- watching the rain through a window
- watching the snow
- lying in front of a log fire
- camping in the country
- walking through the autumn leaves
- watching the stars
- walking through a secret garden
- lying in a warm bed, cuddled up to a puppy

Step 5: Practicing in Real-Life Situations: Rapid Relaxation

Once your child is able to relax quickly and effectively, he or she can begin to practice in real-life situations. It may take two or more weeks of relaxation practice before you move on to this step. At first, it will be too difficult to relax in stressful and frightening situations. It's best for your child to start by practicing the relaxation skills in real-life situations at times that he or she is not frightened. Then gradually you can teach him or her to use relaxation skills in more anxiety-provoking situations.

The relaxation skills that we use in real-life situations involve very rapid tensing and then quick relaxing in a way that is not obvious to other people. These real world relaxation skills can be used in all sorts of situations, such as in the car, at home, out shopping, in the classroom at school, and many other places where fearful events occur. At first, you need to teach your child to use rapid relaxation at home, and then they can begin to apply it in other situations. Rapid relaxation does not use imagery. It focuses on quickly relaxing the muscles and the breathing, to provide control over the bodily symptoms of anxiety. Here are the instructions to give to your child:

> *Now, we need to learn how to relax really quickly in situations when other people are around. Take a really deep breath, tense up the whole body together . . . and hold it tight while we count to five . . . one . . . two . . . three . . . four . . . five. . . . Now breathe*

out slowly and let all the muscles of your body relax together. That's good.

Now, try to stay relaxed. Have a quick check to see whether any parts of your body are tight. And relax those muscles as you breathe out. Try to stay really relaxed. No one knows what you're doing. They don't know that you're using your relaxation skills. But you know that you're in control of your muscles and tension. Think to yourself, "I am in control, I am able to relax. Really relax. I can control my breathing ... in ... and ... out. In and out ... I can control my muscles. Tense and relax. Really relax. No one knows what I'm doing. I can relax. Really relax."

Now it's time for your child to start to practice this rapid relaxation outside the home. Decide together on some times to practice. A good place to start is when you're out together in the car or sitting down having a drink together in a restaurant or at a café. Prompt children to use the rapid relaxation method, and praise them for their efforts. Check how well they were able to relax. Once your child is able to relax in situations outside the home, you can start to encourage him or her to use this skill when facing frightening situations. You can give a prompt to your child to use rapid relaxation as a coping skill. Relaxation methods will be valuable in later chapters of this book when you and your child start to tackle feared situations.

In Summary

The main points that were presented in this chapter include:

- Relaxation is a skill that requires instruction and practice.

- You need to pick the right time for practice.

- Families need to make time for relaxation.

- Relaxation practice needs to become a habit.

- You need to create a relaxing environment in which to practice.

- Parents teach by example.

- Relaxation practice should be enjoyable.

- With children, relaxation sessions need to be short and simple.

- Ultimately, children need to use their relaxation skills in real life situations.

- It helps to keep a record of practice sessions.

- Work through the different relaxation steps with your child.

- Eventually, your child will be able to use relaxation as a coping skill in real-life situations.

Chapter 5

How Can You Help Manage Your Child's Anxiety?

Objectives

By the time you've completed this chapter, you will have a good understanding of:

- the way in which you currently deal with your child's anxiety

- the advantages and disadvantages of some of the most common strategies used by parents to handle their children's anxiety

- an effective step-by-step approach to handling your child's anxiety

Your Current Strategies

There are numerous different ways of handling a child's anxiety. Some of the more common strategies are in the following list. As a general rule, some of these strategies are effective in managing child anxiety and some of them are not. Each strategy will be reviewed in more detail in this chapter. Place a check beside each strategy or strategies that you think are characteristic of the way in which you currently handle your child's anxiety. You'll probably find that you use several of these strategies at different times.

- excessively reassuring a child (for example, repeatedly tell the child that "everything will be all right")
- telling a child exactly how to handle the situation
- empathizing with a child's anxiety by discussing in detail what makes you anxious and afraid
- being tough with a child and not letting him or her avoid the situation
- removing a child from the feared situation or allowing a child to avoid the situation
- prompting a child to independently decide how to cope constructively with his or her anxiety
- ignoring a child's anxiety
- becoming impatient with a child

Can you think of any other strategies that you use in dealing with your child's anxiety? List any that are relevant in the space below:

_____

_____

_____

In case you're beginning to wonder whether the way in which you parent your child is going to be called into question, rest assured—it's not! The above list has been generated with the help of other parents who have been involved with this program in the past. It's not meant to gauge how "good" a parent you are. Rather, it is intended to show that lots of other parents face similar difficulties and often respond to them in similar ways to you.

Being the parent of an anxious child can be really tough, and no doubt there are times when you feel that you just don't know what to do and say in response to your child's anxiety. No doubt there are many times when you feel that nothing that you do or say seems to work. Typically, when an individual is very involved in a particular situation or problem, it's difficult for that person to view the situation in question objectively. Hopefully, this chapter will help you to gain some objectivity in thinking about the strategies that you're currently using to handle your child's anxiety. By carefully considering the advantages and disadvantages associated with each strategy, you'll be able to make informed decisions regarding whether or not a certain strategy is likely to be effective in the long-term with your child.

There are no right or wrong ways of handling a child, and every child and every family are different. However, there are some things that parents can do to reduce the anxiety that their child will experience in the long run. On the other hand, sometimes parents and children slip into a pattern that isn't very helpful for the child's anxiety. We will discuss some of the ways in which different strategies may help to maintain or reduce your child's anxiety. In this way, you'll be in a better position to choose how you want to handle your child.

Unhelpful Ways of Dealing with Anxiety in Children

Excessively Reassuring Your Child

Based on parents' reports, this strategy appears to be very commonly used with anxious children. Examples of ways in which parents attempt to reassure their children include physical affection or closeness, and telling the child that "everything will be all right," and that there is "nothing to be afraid of." Within reason, these are all great strategies, and if they feel right for you, you should continue to use them. It's only when you find yourself constantly having to reassure your child that alarm bells might start ringing. Loving children and giving them comfort, security, and reassurance when they're hurt is an important part of parenting, and we would never say that you should not reassure your child. In fact, too little reassurance can be as bad as too much. Children who never get reassurance or comfort from their parents are likely to feel insecure and alone. But because of their personalities, anxious children are often not able to rely on themselves and will ask for reassurance far more than other children. That's when you can start to get into a vicious circle.

Reassurance is a natural parental response to a child's distress. Unfortunately, to an anxious child, reassurance is like water off a duck's back. It has very little effect and they come back asking for more. More importantly, even if reassurance may help to relieve your child's anxiety a little in the short run, in the long run the more reassurance you give as a parent, the more reassurance your child will demand.

Reassurance is a form of positive attention for your child. This means that every time your child gets anxious and you reassure him or her, you are actually rewarding your child's anxiety. In some cases, this might make the anxiety seem almost worthwhile for the child. At the very least, it can help to teach children that they cannot cope by themselves and that they need you to handle difficult situations. For this reason, you may find that for anxious children, you will actually need to hold off your reassurance even more than you would for nonanxious children, simply so that anxious children are forced to learn that they can do things themselves.

So what do you do when your child does seek help or reassurance? The best strategy is to help teach children how they can come up with answers themselves rather than always expecting you to do it for them. There are two common ways of doing this. One way is described in detail later in this chapter (see "Helpful Ways of Dealing with Anxiety in Children"). Another technique is to prompt your child to use the detective thinking that they should now be getting used to (see chapter 4). In other words, rather than simply giving your child reassurance (e.g. "Don't worry, it'll be all right"), it would be much better to get them to apply their detective thinking to the worry (e.g. "What would Sherlock Holmes say about this? How might you know whether it will be okay?").

When you're dealing with a child who has become used to asking for reassurance a great deal, you may need to begin gradually and then give less and less help over time. For example, if you decide to encourage your child to use his or her own detective thinking rather than coming to you for reassurance, you may need to spend a little time with your child going through the detective thinking the first few times. After a short while, you can gradually expect children to do more and more of the detective thinking for themselves. Eventually, if children come to you seeking reassurance, you should be able simply to tell them to do their own detective thinking about the problem.

If you're going to make a change from always helping your child as much as he or she wants to withdrawing a little, it's very important that you let your child know. A sudden change without explanation might leave your child feeling hurt, unloved, and afraid. No matter how young your child, you should explain clearly what the changes are going to be and why you're making them. It's also a good idea to introduce rewards (and of course lots of praise) when your child successfully solves a problem by him or herself. Finally, it's absolutely essential that you're consistent. No matter how hard it is, it's important not to give in to your child's requests for reassurance (within reason). Don't enter into extended arguments with children. Rather, inform them clearly and calmly that you are confident that they know the answer and you are not going to discuss it any more. Then ignore any further requests for reassurance. Don't forget to reward and praise your child for successful self-reliance (i.e. for not seeking reassurance).

Kurt's Example

Whenever they're going on a family outing, Kurt bugs his - parents with repeated questions about what will be there, who will be there, what they should take, what he should wear, and so on. In the past, Kurt's parents have tried everything to get him to relax and ask fewer questions. Usually, however, they end up answering his questions for a while, eventually losing patience and yelling at him. Finally, Kurt's mother decided that it was time to tackle this problem in a different way (his father was not very interested in the program).

To begin, Kurt's mother sat down with him at a calm time to discuss the issue. She told him that she loved his usual questions and his curiosity, but that when he was worried about things, he would often begin to ask *too* many questions. She explained that she knew he was very smart and that he was now old enough to answer many of his own questions. She said that the next time he began to worry and ask too many questions, she would help him to do his detective thinking to try to come up with his own answers. After that, Kurt's mother explained, she and his father would ignore any further "worry questions." They would be very pleased with him if he could do his own detective thinking and not ask them any worry questions.

A week later, Kurt's family were invited to a family friend's house for lunch. As the time approached, Kurt began with some questions. He was particularly worried about whether he would know anyone and about the possibility that the other kids might not like him. As soon as he began to ask questions, his mother sat down with him and went through his detective thinking with him. She encouraged him to think about how many times he had previously been to family friends and had known people, whether other kids had usually found him likable, what he was likely to think (based on previous experience) of the other children there, and so on. After Kurt had been through the evidence, his mother praised him and went about her work. The next time that Kurt asked a question about the visit, she said to him, "You know that we've already talked about this and done the detective thinking. I know that you have the answers and you don't need me to tell you. If you ask again, I'm not going to answer you, but I am very happy to talk about anything else you would like to discuss." When Kurt asked again, his mother simply ignored the question. When he did not ask any questions for ten minutes, she said, "Kurt, do you realize that you haven't asked me anything about our outing today for the last ten minutes? I'm really proud of how brave you're being. Keep up the good work." Kurt asked no more questions about the visit that day. After the visit, Kurt's parents took him to his favorite restaurant to congratulate him for being so brave.

Being Too Directive

When a child is extremely anxious, some parents will try to take over and direct the child. In other words, they will tell the child exactly what to do, how to behave, and what to say in the anxiety-provoking situation, or they will do things on behalf of their child.

Take George's parents, for instance. George becomes very anxious in social situations with other children. On one particular occasion, George and his father went to the birthday party of a younger cousin. George spent most of the time sitting beside his father and not mixing with the other children. At one point, a clown arrived and began handing out candy. George's father could see that George would love to have some sweets but that he was not going to step forward and ask for any because he was too shy. So his father leapt up and went to the clown to get some sweets for George. George blushed from ear to ear, but he was very pleased with the candy.

The manner in which parents sometimes take over for their anxious children is an excellent example of what we call "a vicious circle." Usually, parents only adopt this strategy after the repeated experience of watching their child feel helpless with anxiety. Most parents don't tell their kids what to do in anxiety-provoking situations because they are naturally bossy. Instead, parents behave in this way because they feel so much for their child when the child becomes gripped by fear. In the short run, this strategy helps to reduce the child's fear and gets them what they want. However, if you think about it, this reliance on parental direction is actually a form of avoidance. In the example of the party, George has learned that he is unable to handle the feared situation himself, and that he can only do it with his father's help. This helps to further reduce his self-confidence.

Even though it can be very painful, it's vitally important that you don't do too much for your child. The bottom line is that children often learn best by being allowed to make their own mistakes. Also, children can only learn that situations aren't dangerous and that they can cope if they are forced to experience the situation. We will discuss this principle in much more detail in the next chapter. For now, it's important for you simply to think about whether you sometimes become too involved with your child's activities.

So how much involvement is "too much"? Unfortunately, there's no simple answer to this question. There is no way to quantify how involved to be and, of course, every parent and child and every situation will be different. What you need to ask yourself is whether you think that you help your child more than other parents and whether your child relies on himself or herself less than other children of the same age. You may need to think about concrete examples of times when your child has appeared helpless and you felt you had to step in. Talk to other parents and ask what they or their child would do in such situations. And above all, ask yourself, "Did I really need to step in? What would have been the worst thing to happen, if I didn't?" As we said earlier, with an anxious child, it's possible that you may need to help less often than you might otherwise.

Permitting or Encouraging Avoidance

Anxious children avoid lots of activities. As a parent, it's hard to continuously nag your child to try everything, so sometimes you might give in to your child's fears and let him or her avoid them. If this happens occasionally, it's understandable. Obviously, in the short run, your child's anxiety and distress will drop and you will also make yourself very popular by allowing your child to get out of doing things that he or she does not want to do. However, if it becomes a common habit, the long-term consequences of permitting and encouraging avoidance in your child are very serious. As long as children continue to avoid, they won't overcome their anxiety. At this point, you don't need to do anything about avoidance, aside from be aware of it. We will discuss how to deal with avoidance in detail in the next two chapters.

Becoming Impatient with Your Child

Unfortunately, as many parents tell us, it's all too easy to become impatient and frustrated with an anxious child. Nothing you do or say seems to help. At times, it can feel as though children are deliberately clinging to their anxiety. Often it feels like "they could do it, if only they would try harder." While it's understandable that you might sometimes lose your patience, obviously becoming angry with your child will only serve to make him or her more frightened and dependent. If you feel yourself losing patience, it is helpful to ask another person (such as your partner) to help or to leave the situation for a short while to gather your thoughts. It can sometimes be useful to try and remind yourself what you are asking your child to do. Imagine having to confront your worst nightmare (perhaps standing naked in front of your colleagues) and you might be able to understand the difficulty that your child is having to face.

Helpful Ways of Dealing with Anxiety in Children

Rewarding Brave, Nonanxious Behavior

All children, no matter how anxious, will at certain times do things that are frightening for them. As a parent, you should look out for any examples of this type of bravery, no matter how small, and reward them. This will make it more likely that they will happen again. Think of it as fanning the small embers of a fire to get it to grow. At first, you need to look for any example of bravery and make a big fuss over it. Later, as your child becomes less anxious, you can reward only the more obvious examples. Make sure you don't set your expectations too high. Remember, what may seem like a small thing to you may be extremely difficult to a nervous child. You will need to make sure you look for behaviors that are brave based on your child's personality, not on anyone else's standards. By pointing to and focusing on successes, you will help your child to build self-confidence as well as help them realize what they are capable of.

In addition to looking for naturally occurring bravery, at times you may want to encourage your child to do things that are a little challenging for him or her. Again, this needs to be rewarded. We will discuss this strategy in much more detail in the next chapter.

Rewards can fall into two broad types—material and nonmaterial. Material rewards are the ones most of us think of immediately. These might include money, food, stickers, or toys. The child is given the reward, say a small toy, after the brave action is noticed. Nonmaterial rewards include praise, attention, and interest from the parent. Parental attention is an extremely powerful reward. Most children, especially younger children, will do almost anything for the approval and praise of their parents. Spending extra time with your child (e.g. playing a game or going for a bike ride) is a great way to reward them for brave, nonanxious behavior. Whenever possible, we suggest the use of nonmaterial rewards because they have the added benefit of giving your child a sense of security and self-esteem.

It's also important to keep your rewards varied. If your child keeps getting the same reward over and over, it will very quickly lose its impact.

There are several points to remember when using rewards:

- In order to be effective, rewards must be meaningful to the child. There is no point rewarding a child with something he or she doesn't like. The easiest way to make sure that the child will work for the reward is to discuss it with your child. Find out what he or she wants most at this moment.

- Communicate with your child about the rewards. There is no point showering rewards on children if they think the rewards came for no reason. It's important that children know exactly why they're getting the reward and how they can get it again. Praise should be clear and specific. You want children to know exactly what they have done that you liked and want them to repeat in the future. For example, saying "David, you were able to go by yourself with Mrs. Jones into class this morning, instead of needing me to come in with you. I was really proud of you," is much more useful than saying, "You were a good boy today, David."

- The rewards must be in keeping with the activity, and you need to make sure that you give the child a reward that is the right size for the difficulty of the activity. For example, if your child is terrified of dogs and has just spent the last half hour with the neighbor's dog, which she or he has never approached before, it's not fair to give only a small token or two minutes of your time. On the other hand, if your child has done something that was only slightly difficult, you're leaving yourself with nowhere to go if you reward them with a new television.

- Most importantly, rewards must be given as soon as possible after the brave action has occurred, and they must be delivered if promised. Consistency is essential for effective parenting. Children will learn very quickly to stop trusting their parent's word if they find that promises are not delivered. If you promise your child a reward, it must be delivered. Similarly, rewards lose their effectiveness the later they are given. If your child does something brave on Monday and you give them a small reward the following Saturday, the whole impact will have been lost. For maximum impact, the reward should be delivered immediately. That is why your own time and attention can be so much better than buying a gift. Of course, there will be times when delivering an immediate reward is just not practical. For example, you may decide to reward your child by going skiing together. Obviously, this can't be done immediately, and may need to wait until the weekend. In this case, it is useful to give some sort of interim reward. For example, you may make up a small voucher that clearly says the reason for earning the voucher on it, and have your child exchange it at the weekend for the ski trip. At the very least, if the reward is delayed, you need to make an immediate fuss and give attention to the brave act and make it very clear that the later reward and the brave act are connected.

- If you have other children, you may find that they become resentful of the extra attention and rewards that your anxious child is getting. One way around this might be to introduce a reward system for all children in the family. You can introduce a star chart where each child can earn rewards, although the rewards might be earned by different behaviors for each child. In this way, you can build bravery in all your children if needed, or you could use the rewards for your other children to increase helpful habits such as obedience, cleaning teeth, tidying their rooms, and so on.

Ignoring Behaviors That You Don't Want

This is really the flip side of the previous strategy. It involves removing your attention from your child's anxious behavior and attending again (and praising) when the anxious behavior has stopped. The idea is that when you notice a behavior that you are not happy with (for example, your child repeatedly complaining about feeling sick before school), you need to stop any interaction with your child as long as she or he is doing that behavior (complaining). Of course, it is essential that your child understand exactly why you are ignoring him or her and exactly what she or he needs to do in order to regain your attention. Using this strategy should be immediately followed by specific praise for something good that the child is doing (e.g. complaining stops for one minute). As we discussed previously, ignoring is a particularly useful strategy for dealing with reassurance seeking. This strategy must always be used carefully and only in relation to a specific behavior. It's important that your child understands that it is the particular behavior in which he or she is engaging that is unacceptable to you and not his or her general character.

Preventing Avoidance

As we discussed in chapter 4, avoiding feared situations is one of the main causes for anxiety in children. By avoiding feared situations, children never learn that they can cope with their anxiety, that the situation is not really dangerous, and that they are stronger than they had realized. Obviously, you must be satisfied that your child is actually capable of coping in the anxiety-provoking situation. You should not force your child to do something that he or she is not actually able to do. For example, it may not be helpful to encourage your child to enter a singing contest if his or her singing isn't a strong suit. Doing this would set the child up for failure, and would only strengthen the original anxiety. In the same way, it is not helpful to force your child to do something that really is terrifying for him or her. However, you will need to push to some degree so that your child starts to do things that are slightly difficult and gradually builds up the degree of difficulty. Exactly how to do this will be discussed in the next chapter.

Communicating Your Empathy Effectively

When you are talking with your child about the things that make him or her anxious, it's important that you express your empathy and understanding in a calm and relaxed manner. Children need to feel listened to, understood, and supported, but it's equally important that they're encouraged to constructively solve the problem of their anxiety rather than focusing on how bad they feel.

Prompting Children to Cope Constructively

Parents who use this strategy typically prompt their children to think for themselves about how to constructively handle an anxiety-provoking situation. This is quite different to parents who tell their children exactly what to do in the anxiety-provoking situation (see George's example).

George's Example

George is highly anxious about a debate he has to take part in at school. He is very upset and imagines the worst possible outcome. George is sure that he will make a mess of his speech and look like a complete idiot. He complains that he has a headache and that his stomach hurts.

George's mom comes and sits down with him. She says to him, "George, I can understand that you feel a bit worried about the debate. But the fact is that you have to do it for class, and at the moment, you're just not helping yourself. You're saying a lot of negative things about how things are going to go, and that must be making you feel worse. Plus, you're talking yourself into feeling sick. What you're doing right now isn't making you feel any better, is it?" George agrees with his mother. She then goes on, "Okay. So, what can you do that might help? What can you do that would make you feel better?" George answers this by saying that staying away from school on the day of his team's debate would help him feel better. His mom points out that George's teacher would probably just postpone his team's debate until he came back to school, and George will have to do more public speaking tasks now that he is in high school, and that if he puts it off now, the next time will be even harder. George can see the logic of this, especially the first point. He suggests that maybe if he practiced the speech with his mom, he might feel better about it. She praises him for coming up with a constructive way of dealing with his anxiety and agrees to practice with him.

In this example, the parent is prompting the child to come up with his own solutions. She is not encouraging him to rely on her by directly intervening. Instead, she is encouraging him to take responsibility for managing his own anxiety in a constructive manner. At the same time, she is firmly not allowing him to avoid the debate.

Encouraging your child to use the detective approach to evaluate the realistic probability of his or her negative, worrying thoughts being true is an important component of this strategy. Prompting your child to independently decide how to cope constructively with his or her anxiety is a good long-term strategy, because it involves showing faith in your child's abilities. You would be surprised at how often children are able to rise to meet their parents' expectations. If you believe that your child possesses the ability to overcome challenges and to solve problems, he or she is more likely to believe this too.

Modeling Brave, Nonanxious Behavior

Children learn how to behave by observing others (most significantly, their parents). Thus, as a parent, everything that you do or say has added significance because you are serving as a model for your child. The very best type of model is a "coping model," that is, models who demonstrate that they experience difficulties and also that they cope constructively with these difficulties. This type of model is more effective than one who apparently never experiences any difficulties. If you believe that you have a problem with anxiety yourself, it may be worth seeking help so that you can begin to model more effective coping to your child.

What to Do When Your Child Becomes Frightened

You may be wondering at this point, how do I stop my child from feeling anxious at those times when he or she suddenly becomes very scared and refuses to do something? The simple answer is, "You don't!" It's not possible to take away all anxiety from a child. We all feel anxious at times, and we all need to learn how to deal with it. Even though it's really hard to see it in our own children, as parents, we sometimes have to accept that our children will feel anxious. The good news however, is that there are some things you can try to help reduce your child's anxiety.

1. Summarize what your child has said. Check the accuracy of your understanding of the problem, that is, make sure that you know

what he or she actually means. Communicate your empathy with your child in a sympathetic but calm way.

2. Summarize the choices open to the child at this point. On the one hand, the child can continue to feel anxious and upset, and to behave in an anxious manner. On the other hand, the child can choose to do something to reduce his or her anxiety.

3. Make sure you don't just take over the task for children. Rather, help them come up with their own suggestions of ways to reduce the anxiety and feel better. Ask children to brainstorm all the possible ways in which their anxiety might be reduced. Praise the child for the ideas that they've generated. Even if the ideas are not actually very useful, praise them for effort. The fact that they're engaging with you in the process of trying to constructively reduce their anxiety is a very positive and important step.

4. Go through each idea or strategy that the child has generated, one by one. For each idea, ask the child, "What would happen if you did this?" If the child does not identify obvious consequences of a strategy, gently point them out to him or her (for instance, you might say, "I wonder if _____ would happen if you did _____ to make yourself feel better. What do you think?"). Remember, your overriding goal is to encourage approach solutions rather than avoidant solutions. Praise the child for trying to generate likely outcomes or consequences for each strategy.

5. Encourage your child to think of his or her detective character and to use his or her detective thinking.

6. Prompt the child to select the strategy that is most likely to result in a positive outcome and least likely to result in a negative outcome. Remind your child to remember the evidence he or she has generated with the detective thinking.

Jack's Example

Maggie and Dan are going out to dinner to celebrate their wedding anniversary. Their nine-year-old son, Jack, is extremely anxious about being separated from them, particularly at night. He is crying and clinging to his parents, begging them not to go out.

Step 1: Maggie and Dan sit down with Jack and find out what the problem is.

Maggie:	Jack, we can see that you're very upset about the idea of us going out. Can you tell us exactly what it is that's worrying you?
Jack:	I don't know. I just don't want you to go.
Dan:	Okay, we know that you don't want us to go. But we need you to tell us why. What is it that you're afraid will happen if we go out?
Jack:	You might be in an accident and be hurt.
Maggie:	[Maggie summarizes and checks her understanding of what Jack has said] So, you don't want us to go out because you think that we might be in an accident and get hurt. Is that right, Jack? Is that why you're so upset?
Jack:	Yes.

Step 2: Maggie and Dan present Jack with his choices.

Dan:	Okay, Jack, your mother and I *are* going out tonight. And it's really up to you how you deal with that. You can keep on doing what you're doing right now and feel really bad. Or, you can try and do something to cope with the bad feelings that you're having. Mom and I would really like to help you cope with the bad feelings. Are you willing to give that a try?
Jack:	I want you to stay with me at home. If you stay, I won't have any bad feelings.
Maggie:	Jack, you heard your dad. We're not going to stay at home with you tonight. The decision you have to make is what you're going to do about how you're feeling right now. How about you work with us and we'll try and come up with a plan to make you feel better?
Jack:	I guess ...
Dan:	Good boy.

Steps 3 and 4: Maggie and Dan prompt Jack to generate suggestions as to how he might cope with his anxiety (that is, what he might do to make himself feel better). Jack is praised for his effort.

Maggie:	Okay, Jack. We need to think of as many things as possible that you can do that might make you feel better. What do you think you could do?

Jack: What do you mean? I don't understand.

Dan: Well, for instance, you're worried about us going out because you're saying to yourself that if we go out, we might have an accident. Maybe instead, you could watch a video and take your mind off your worries. Do you see what I mean?

Jack: I could take your car keys and hide them. Then you wouldn't be able to go.

Maggie: Well, that's one idea. At this stage, we'll write down all the ideas and then we can decide on one later on.

Jack: I could go and watch my videos to take my mind off things.

Dan: Great, Jack. What else could you do?

Jack: I could write down that thing about you and Mom being good drivers, so that I can remember it later.

Maggie: You mean your detective thinking—that's really excellent, Jack. You're trying really hard and coming up with some good ideas. Can you think of anything else?

   Step 5: Maggie and Dan prompt Jack to identify the likely consequences or outcomes of each of the coping strategies generated.

Dan: Right. Now Jack, we've got a few different ideas written down here as to what you might do to make yourself feel better about us going out. Let's go through them one at a time and find out what would happen if you actually did each of these things. First of all, there was the idea that you hide the car keys? What do you think would happen if you did that?

Jack: You might stay home?

Dan: You know Jack, I think that if you did that, it's probably more likely that we'd send you to your room and call a taxi to take us out to dinner.

Jack: Yeah, I guess.

Dan: How about your idea about watching a video? What would happen if you did that?

Jack: I'd have fun and I wouldn't be thinking about you and Mom.

Dan: And how about your idea of writing down that your mom and I are good drivers? What do you think would happen if you did that?

Jack: It would remind me that you probably wouldn't have an accident, and I might feel better.

Maggie: Okay, that's the end of our list. Well done, Jack, you're doing a really excellent job of helping yourself get over your bad feelings.

Step 6: Maggie and Dan prompt Jack to choose the most positive and least negative solution.

Dan: Okay, now the last thing we need to do is to pick one of these ideas. Have a look at the list and the things that would probably happen if you chose each idea. Which one do you think would have the best results for you?

Jack: Well, that's easy. It would be my idea of watching the video. Plus, I could also write down something about you and Mom being good drivers, to remind myself not to worry.

Maggie: I think that's an excellent choice. Well done, Jack. Your dad and I are very proud of you for being able to figure out how to cope with your worry in a helpful way.

Note: Assuming that Jack handled his anxiety in a useful way and allowed Dan and Maggie to go out without difficulty, they would praise his efforts the next morning and might organize a special reward, such as playing a favorite game with his parents, to acknowledge his bravery.

Practice

For the situation in which your child becomes most anxious, try to jot down some ideas for each step in the approach outlined above. As you go through this process, try to identify the problems you are most likely to encounter at each step.

The situation is: _____

Step 1: _____

Step 2: _____

Step 3: _____

Step 4: _____

Step 5: _____

Step 6: _____

Step 7: _____

In Summary

- There are many different ways of handling your child's anxiety. Some of these are more effective than others.

- Some methods tend to be less effective and may even increase your child's anxiety. These include: excessively reassuring the child, being too directive, permitting or encouraging avoidance, and becoming impatient with your child.

- The most useful strategies for handling anxiety in children include: not allowing avoidance, helping the child to independently manage his or her anxiety in a constructive manner, and reducing reassurance-seeking by ignoring this behavior.

- When your child becomes anxious about a future event, there are several steps you can follow to help your child to come up with some constructive solutions.

Chapter 6

Reality Testing

Objectives

By the time you have finished this chapter, you should understand:

- why reality testing is important

- how to plan a step-by-step reality testing plan with your child

- how you can help your child put reality testing into practice

Understanding Reality Testing

The realistic thinking steps from chapter 3 taught your child different ways to think about things that worry him or her. This is an important first step in managing anxiety. However, learning new ways of thinking about a situation is not enough by itself to overcome worries and fears. Thinking realistically is not much use if the old ways of behaving don't change as well. It's time now for your child to try out his or her new ability to deal with fears and worries in real situations.

Reality testing is a way to help children overcome their fears by facing up to the very things they are scared of. It's mostly a commonsense procedure, and you'll probably find that you've tried something like it before. The difference here is that we will put it into an overall anxiety-management plan, and we'll show you how to be more structured in the way you approach this strategy. Reality testing is carried out in a step-by-step fashion so that it isn't overwhelming for your child. In this way, your child will experience difficult situations gradually and learn to cope with them. Being encouraged to try things that are frightening and learning to cope will give your child confidence and help to break the pattern of automatically responding with fear and worry.

Avoiding Fears Doesn't Help

There's an old story of two men walking along the street and one man keeps stopping every few steps to bang his head on the sidewalk. Finally, his friend can't stand it anymore and says, "Will you *stop* hitting your head on the sidewalk?" The first man answers, "I can't, it keeps the crocodiles away." His friend says, "But there are no crocodiles here!" The first man smiles and says, "See."

Anxious children will avoid many apparent dangers that just aren't very likely to happen when we look at them rationally. However, by continuing to avoid, the child never learns that his or her behavior has nothing to do with the outcome. Just think of the children, for example, who are frightened of being killed while sleeping and so want to sleep with their mom and dad every night. We all know that the chance that they will be killed while sleeping is almost zero. But by sleeping with their parents every night, they never actually learn this. Logically convincing themselves that they won't be killed by use of detective thinking is the first step. But this is not enough. Children must actually face their fear to really convince themselves that being killed at night just won't happen.

Avoiding worry actually strengthens the anxious beliefs, making it increasingly difficult for children to do things. Most anxious children have developed ways to avoid situations where they may become anxious. Sometimes these avoidance strategies can be very subtle and so habitual that even parents can be unaware of them. Reality testing gives your child opportunities to practice different ways of behaving and learn that he or she really is able to cope with the fear.

The same ideas apply to all types of fears, whether they are fears of being separated from parents, fears of specific objects (e.g. heights or spiders), or excessive worrying about social situations or performance in a school test. The particular things that you face up to might differ, but the basic principles remain the same.

Let's look at an example of how you might try to overcome a fear of your own using reality testing. Suppose you were afraid of public speaking and you wanted to become more comfortable with this so that you could take a promotion at work that involved giving talks to large groups of people. Naturally, you would begin by doing your realistic thinking—what is it you are worried about, what is the evidence that this would happen, and so on. You would also practice relaxation so that you can try to relax before and during your talks. But these two techniques alone will not be enough. You also need to face your fears.

To begin with, you might decide to present a short speech to your family. This would perhaps be a little frightening because it might seem silly, but it shouldn't be too hard. Once you've done this step (perhaps more than once), you might decide that you're now ready to present a short talk to a group of friends. After this, you might practice doing readings and introducing speakers at your local club. The whole time you're doing these steps, you would be practicing your realistic thinking and applying your relaxation techniques.

After a few weeks of practicing these easier steps, you should find your confidence starting to build. Your next step might then involve presenting a few practice talks to your work colleagues. At the same time, you might join a public speaking club and practice giving weekly talks to the club members. Finally, you would grab that promotion and begin to give talks as part of your new job. Even here, you could break things down by organizing your schedule so that your first talks are to smaller and less important groups and your later talks are the really tough ones. By gradually and systematically building up to your final goal in this way, you will become used to public speaking and will learn that you can cope and that the terrible things you may have imagined before are just not very likely. Over a period of weeks (or even months) you will find yourself becoming less and less worried about presenting in public. This is reality testing.

Exactly the same principles apply when you begin to do reality testing with your child. For example, let's think of a child who is afraid of going to sleep in the dark and wants the light on in his or her room every night. To do reality testing, you might first get the child to go to sleep with a light on in the hall that is still fairly bright. If this is not too big a step, the child will most likely agree. After several nights, you may convince the child to go to sleep with a light on in the room across the hall. Then, after a few nights, the child might agree to try a small, fairly dull lamp in the hall outside. Eventually, the child could try going to sleep with the only light being a very faint one, in a distant room. Finally, the child will go to sleep without the light on at all. At each step the child will undoubtedly be a little anxious. But by gradually reducing the light in this way and having small enough steps, the child can reach the final goal without ever having to face extreme fear.

How Does Reality Testing Work?

Reality testing is a step-by-step way to beat fears. With your help, your child will work out a step-by-step plan to beat the fear. Your child will attempt each step in turn, beginning with the least difficult and working up to situations that are the most worrying.

Every step of reality testing is more proof that children can beat the fears. They will feel proud of their success as they conquer each step, but they will need your encouragement to keep going. A system of rewards can be negotiated between you and your child to provide extra incentives to keep trying. To remind yourself about the ways to use rewards, see the section on rewards in chapter 5.

Children learn from reality testing that even if they feel worried, they can cope. During the steps of reality testing, children will have to experience some situations that make them feel worried. This is important to help children learn that, although they may have started off feeling uncomfortable and worried, the bad things they feared did not actually happen. By doing this, your child learns that he or she can tolerate some feelings of worry and that this doesn't stop them from doing things. After all, none of us can go through life without ever feeling anxious.

Practice is the key to success. It's not enough to practice a step just once. Your child will have to repeat each step over and over until the situation no longer causes a lot of anxiety.

How You Can Help

Anxious children lack confidence in their ability to manage certain situations. They may believe that they are less capable or weaker than other children. Children's past experience may make them reluctant to try something new or something they may have "failed" at before. You're going to have to encourage your child to try to do things that will not be easy. You'll need to be sympathetic and understanding, but at the same time, you'll have to be tough. This won't be easy. But remind yourself that it is for your child's good in the long run. At times, it may help to read over chapter 5 on child management.

Believe That Your Child Can Do It

You may be worried about your child's capacity to tolerate anxiety and discomfort. For example, you might feel that he or she is more sensitive than other children. Children can pick up subtle messages from parents about how capable they are or how difficult certain tasks may be. For this reason, it's important that you don't let your worries show. Be positive about what your child is trying to change.

Are You Worried Too?

As a parent, it can be very difficult to know when to be sympathetic and help out children and when to ask them to try a little harder. This can be extra difficult for parents who may have similar fears. You know that it is good for them to do it, but you may also feel empathy with the worries children have and feel inclined to protect them. If you feel like this, it's understandable. But you'll have to try and separate your own concerns from those of your child. It may help to do your own realistic thinking about the problem.

When your child begins to do reality testing, you may well find this quite difficult to face. There will be times when you will be sending your child out to face some pretty difficult situations and to possibly become quite frightened. At these times, many parent feel guilty and torn. If this is a risk for you, you need to try to put some safeguards into place to help you through this part of the program. First, remind yourself that encouraging children to face their fears is good for them, and it is the only way they will overcome their fears.

Next, brainstorm some ways in which you might help yourself feel better at those times when you feel bad. For example, you might write out a detective thinking sheet for your own beliefs and worries at these times and read it over to remind yourself of the more realistic beliefs. Or you might make sure you have plenty of work to get into to distract yourself from your guilty thoughts. Alternately, you might be able to ask for support from your partner or a good friend. These people might be able to remind you that you are doing the right thing and that your child will not "break" or "hate you" for what he or she is going through.

At the end of the day, these feelings are completely understandable, but they need to be overcome for the good of your child.

Be Clear about What You Expect

It's important to be clear in your mind about what the reasonable expectations are for children of your child's age and for your child particularly. Your child will be best helped if you're clear on what you expect him or her to be able to do and how much you will help. For example, it would be unrealistic to expect a six-year-old child who is afraid of being away from his or her parents to stay home alone in the evening. But it would be quite reasonable for a fifteen-year-old to do this. In a similar way, there might be different expectations for children in different areas. For example, expecting your child to walk home alone from the bus stop might be quite reasonable in certain neighborhoods but not in others. Talk to other parents, your child's teacher, or a therapist if you're unsure about what you should reasonably expect from your child. In addition, if you have a partner or someone else who also cares for your child, make sure you sort out these expectations together so that you are in agreement about what your child should do. It's very difficult for children to learn not to fear certain things if they're getting different messages from their caretakers.

Steps to Teach Children Reality Testing

Teaching children the ideas of reality testing involves the following steps, which we will discuss in detail.

Step 1: Explaining Reality Testing to Children

The first step in conducting reality testing with your child is to explain clearly and simply the purpose of the exercise. It's important that your child is a willing and active participant in the process, or you'll be fighting an uphill battle. Naturally, the way in which you explain reality testing will vary a little depending on your child's age.

A useful way of explaining reality testing to children is to tell them a story of a child facing a problem and ask them to suggest some ideas on how they could help the child overcome his or her fears.

A good example might be to describe a child who is frightened of swimming in deep water. Ask children what they might suggest to that child to help him or her get used to going into the water. Most children are pretty good at coming up with a commonsense plan. Hopefully, children will be able to come up with a plan where the child would begin with a low-fear step (for example, going into water up to his or her knees). If children don't come up with a sensible approach, you will need to prompt them. Next, the child should gradually begin to move deeper and deeper into the water. This should be done gradually, while allowing time for the child to relax and get used to each step. Hopefully, children will understand that the frightened child will need to experience a little bit of fear, but by moving through each step gradually and getting used to each step along the way, he or she would eventually reach the final goal without too much discomfort.

Here are a few other examples you could try:

- Katie hates heights, but really wants to go to her best friend's birthday party in a restaurant on top of a very tall building.

- Jeff won't play in the park or the garden in case there's a spider there.

- Adriana is afraid of the dark and still sleeps with the light on.

Of course, many children, especially older children, will be more anxious about social- and performance-based fears (e.g. worrying about being judged badly by other people when speaking in public or meeting new people). Explaining the reality testing ideas can be harder for these problems. It's best to start by explaining the ideas with a simple problem such as a specific fear of dogs, heights, or spiders first. Then you can move on to other fears that young people commonly experience, such as those given in these examples:

- Sonia worries about calling people on the phone.

- Tony has to give a speech to his whole school in a month, and he's terrified.

- Jack gets nervous when he has to play tennis in front of a lot of people.

Some children will be a little concerned about what they will be expected to try and how difficult it may be. This is to be expected. Anxious children's usual behavior when faced with something that makes them anxious is to lower their level of worry by avoiding the situation. You can use the examples given to point out to children that if they want to overcome their fears, they will have to get a little anxious. However, by doing it in small steps, it should never get too scary. And they will be earning rewards!

Step 2: Making a Fears and Worries List

Once your child understands the idea of reality testing in principle, the next step is to apply these ideas to his or her own specific difficulties. To begin, you and your child will need to sit and brainstorm all the different things that he or she is afraid of. It may help to use the "fears and worries list" we have included. The list should aim to record a number of different situations and activities that your child finds frightening and usually avoids. For example, items such as big dogs, meeting new people, and spending time away from you, could all be included. For some children there may only be one fear, while for others there will be many. No doubt, you will have many suggestions and you'll need to make sure that your child covers as much as possible. But it's important that your child is involved in the exercise, so encourage him or her to come up with the ideas first if possible. Try to make this a fun game, seeing how many things you can list. Children may need reminding of specific situations where they may have been anxious rather than coming up with a general concept such as fear of separation. It's important that this is not seen as a list of failings, but as a list of things they would like to be able to do.

At this stage the idea is to get your child involved and brainstorming. Don't worry if the suggestions are not real or even sensible. They can be fixed later. Also, don't worry if it doesn't cover everything. The list can be added to later—it's a working reminder of what your child wants to change. It may help to generate items if you divide the list into things that are really hard, moderately hard, and not too hard.

You might find that your child isn't able to come up with fears or may even suddenly claim now to have no problems at all. It's not uncommon for anxious children to want to deny any difficulties. We call this "faking good," and it usually happens because your child wants to appear "perfect" both to you and to him or herself. If you believe that your child is avoiding acknowledging his or her fears, don't nag. Begin by suggesting one or two situations that were difficult recently. Focus on the lower level fears, and remind your child that you will tackle those first and then come back to the list. Some children may avoid some areas of difficulty, for example social fears, but focus on others. Acknowledge that they're working on one area and plan to try the other, more difficult problems later. As they succeed on easier problems, your child will gain the confidence to try to beat some other worries. If your child still denies having any difficulties, challenge them to try certain things anyway. For example, you might say something like, "I think you are a little afraid of _____ , so why don't we put this down and if you are not, then you can prove to me that I am wrong."

Fears and Worries List

These things are **really** hard to do		Worry Scale 0–10
These things are hard to do		Worry Scale 0–10
These things make me a little worried		Worry Scale 0–10

Lashi's Example

Lashi had many worries, and they seemed to be getting worse, upsetting everyone in the family. Lashi and her mother made a list of the main things she worried about. Her mom chose a quiet time when she and Lashi could talk about the worries. At first Lashi thought everything worried her equally but, when talking with her mother, she was able to sort the worries into groups. Writing it down can make the fears seem more manageable.

Lashi's Fears and Worries List

These things are really hard to do	staying with a sitter while Mom goes out for the night 9
	having an injection 10
	Mom being late home or to pick me up 9
	burglars 10
	sleeping in my own bed 8
These things are hard to do	going to school 6
	going to the doctor's with Mom 5
	hearing strange noises at night 7
	being in the dark 6
	staying over at Dad's place 5
These things make me a little worried	being in a different room at home than Mom 2
	going to a friend's house after school 4
	visiting my grandparents' with Mom 1
	visiting Dad's place for the afternoon 2

Using this list of fears and worries, Lashi and her parents could choose which worries to start with to make a step-by-step plan to fight her fears. The fears seemed to fall into three main groups: 1) being away from her mom either at home or when she went to her father's; 2) going to other peoples houses or to school; and 3) specific fears such as dealing with the dark, sleeping by herself, and going to the doctor and getting injections.

Step 3: Working Out a Step-by-Step Plan

Once you've listed as many fears as possible, the next step is to organize the fears into a practical plan. The aim is to have one or more "stepladders"—that is, lists of fears that are practical and organized so that they contain a number of steps going from the easiest to the hardest.

You will find that some of the fears that you have recorded on the fears and worries list are small practical steps in and of themselves. For example, the item from Lashi's list, "visiting grandparents with Mom," is rated as a low level worry and is practical and doable. On the other hand, some of the items on your list will be much broader and larger. For example, from Lashi's list the item "being in the dark" is quite vague and broad, because Lashi's level of fear might be very different depending, for example, on whether she was inside or outside, which room she was in, what time it was, how dark it was, and so on. The items that are practical and doable can be left as is. However, the items that are broad and a little vague need to be rewritten so they are much more specific. This might involve breaking them down into several smaller steps. For example, the item "being in the dark" could be broken down into several different items, such as "being in my room with the light down low," "being in my room with the light off in the early evening," "being in my room later at night with the light off," "being in the far room with the light off," "standing outside the back door with the light off," and "standing at the end of the garden with the light off."

The next step is to ask your child to list the different activities in order of difficulty. In other words, look at the list and ask your child which item on the list she or he would find the easiest to do. Then ask which is the next easiest, and so on, all the way up to the hardest. Once you've organized the items from the easiest to the hardest, you and your child will have a stepladder.

If your child has a lot of different fears, you may find it easier to create several stepladders. Each stepladder would contain items that logically go together and are relating to the same overall category. For example, you may have one stepladder for being away from parents, another for mixing with people, and a third for sleeping in the dark.

In creating stepladders, you'll need to make sure that you and your child have come up with steps that aren't too far apart. The eventual idea will be for your child to begin with the first step on the ladder and practice that item until she or he feels relatively comfortable with it. Then, she or he will need to move on to the next item up the ladder, and so on. If the steps are too far apart—if the next step is too much of a jump for your child—he or she may not be able to do it and could lose confidence. One way to create steps is to take a large sheet of paper and draw a figure of the child on one side and across the page a picture of them doing what they are most fearful of. Explain to your child that you are going to work out a plan together to overcome this fear. Parents and children can brainstorm together all the possible things children could do to train themselves to be able reach their goal in small steps.

The best way to create smaller steps to reach a goal is to think about several different ways that a child can face a situation. For example, a situation such as asking directions from a stranger on the street can include many different features that will result in quite different levels of anxiety. Directions could be asked from a male or a female, from an older person or a younger person, or from a single person, a couple of people, or a group of people. Each of these variations would most likely produce very different levels of anxiety for a shy child and each child will be different. By brainstorming about these variations, you can produce a large number of steps that your child can then place into order of difficulty and put onto a stepladder.

Another important consideration in creating a stepladder is to choose items that are doable. After all, your child is eventually going to be asked to do each item on the list. Look over the list and eliminate any steps that are off-track or not easily possible. For example, in dealing with a fear of heights, climbing to the top of Mt. Everest might really help, but it's not very likely to happen.

We have included a fighting fear worksheet to help you to record your stepladders. Make as many copies as you need for extra stepladders. This sheet has six steps, but you can have more or less. There is no set number of steps to be included but there should be enough to provide plenty of opportunities for practice. It is more effective to have a larger number of smaller steps to reinforce the learning, rather than a few large ones. Large steps and big jumps in the level of difficulty between items must be avoided. Each step should be very clear with details of time to be spent, the place, and what is to be achieved. Use everyday activities to give your child opportunities to really do lots of practice. Tasks that are too elaborate or difficult to organize, demanding special efforts from parents, will rarely be done despite good intentions.

Lashi's Example

Lashi and her mom came up with a number of different areas that she was frightened of, including sleeping overnight at various people's places (including her father's), sleeping by herself at night in the dark, staying home with a sitter while her mother goes out, and going to school. To help organize all of her fears more easily, Lashi and her mother decided to create separate stepladders for each of these different areas. We show below part of Lashi's stepladder for learning to stay home while her mom goes out.

Lashi's goal is to be able to stay at home with a sitter without worrying about her mom being out.

Fighting Fears—Step by Step

I want to _____

_____

Step 6 _____

_____

My reward _____

Step 5 _____

_____

My reward _____

Step 4 _____

_____

My reward _____

Step 3 _____

_____

My reward_____

Step 2 _____

_____

My reward _____

Step 1 _____

_____

My reward _____

Lashi's Step-by-Step Reality Testing Plan

1. Staying home with Dad while Mom goes out for ten minutes

2. Staying home with Grandma while Mom goes out for thirty minutes

3. Staying home with Dad while Mom goes out for the afternoon

4. Staying home with Grandma while Mom goes out for most of the day

5. Staying home with a sitter while Mom goes out for the afternoon

6. Staying home with a sitter while Mom goes out for most of the day

7. Staying home with Dad while Mom goes out for the evening (a few hours)

8. Staying home with Grandma while Mom goes out for the night (until late)

9. Staying home with a sitter while Mom goes out for a few hours in the evening

10. Staying home with a sitter while Mom goes out for the night (until late)

George's Perfectionism

Part of George's shyness also extended to a perfectionistic streak. George was so worried about what others thought of him that he tried not to make any mistakes. As a result, he often worried extensively about whether he had said or done the wrong thing and he often redid his schoolwork many times in order to get it just right. Below is part of one stepladder that George made up to tackle this problem.

George's goal is to not be bothered by making mistakes at school.

Step-by-Step Reality Testing Plan

1. Intentionally calling Mark (a close friend) by the wrong name

2. Not brushing hair before school

3. Ruling a wobbly line on a page and leaving it there

4. Not checking an essay for mistakes before handing it in

5. Making a deliberate mistake in a science project

6. Intentionally handing in an essay with several spelling mistakes

7. Answering a question in class when not 100 percent sure of the answer

8. Intentionally returning library books three days late

9. Deliberately giving the wrong answer to a question in class

10. Not doing the correct homework

George's Fear of Public Speaking

Being very shy, one of George's worst fears was speaking in front of other people. The following stepladder was designed to tackle this problem. George did not begin work on this stepladder until after he had done several steps on most of his other stepladders. This was both because public speaking was not a very important goal for George, and also because it was a harder topic to tackle than several of his other goals.

George's goal is presenting a talk to the class.

Step-by-Step Reality Testing Plan

1. Preparing a talk—not to be delivered

2. Preparing a short talk and practicing alone and taping it

3. Giving a short talk to parents

4. Giving the talk again to parents and deliberately forgetting something

5. Giving the talk to grandparents and mispronouncing a word

6. Giving the talk to aunts and deliberately dropping notes

7. Giving the talk to friends and family

8. Giving a longer talk to friends and family

9. Asking a question of the teacher in class

10. Giving a two-minute report to the whole class

11. Giving a longer talk to the class

12. Making an announcement to the whole school

Kurt's Fears about Germs

Kurt is worried about several things, including getting dirt on his hands or being contaminated in any way. Below is part of one of Kurt's stepladders to tackle his fear of germs and his need to wash extensively to cleanse himself. In cases such as this, you need to think of the washing behavior as a type of avoidance—that is, an avoidance of having any germs on the body by washing them off. Therefore, this behavior needs to be stopped in order for the reality testing to work. What you need to do is to get your child to learn that even without washing, dirt on his or her body will not hurt him or her. Children with these problems also need to do more in their reality testing than most of us would usually do in our daily lives. For example, one step might involve urinating a few drops on hands and then not washing it off. Most of us would never want to do this, but it is not actually dangerous and to learn this lesson, children with these fears will need to do this until it no longer scares them. As we said earlier, if you have a child with these types of problems, we strongly urge you to seek additional guidance from a mental health professional.

Kurt's goal is to play without being bothered by worries about germs and dirt.

Step-by-Step Reality Testing Plan

1. Sit on the bench in the local park for five minutes

2. Play basketball with Dad

3. Sit on the grass and put my hands on grass for five minutes

4. Go to football game with Dad and sit directly on seats and touch them with hands

5. Go and play at Connor's house and not wash before dinner [Kurt felt that Connor's parents did not clean their house]

6. Catch public train and touch seats and handrails

7. Play with neighbor with skin problem and then not wash

8. Take off shoes after playing outside and then eat and drink something (no washing between)

9. Use the toilet before eating, then eat (no washing between)

10. Spill some drops of urine onto hands in morning, let them dry, then do not wash for rest of day

Note: Each step is to be completed without Kurt washing, showering, or changing his clothes. Kurt is to change his day clothes only at night (unless his parents deem otherwise), shower once per day, and wash his hands only when his parents agree they are clearly dirty.

Step 4: Motivation and Rewards

Asking children to do reality testing can be like asking someone to have a tooth removed without anesthetic. Reality testing will be hard work for your child and, at times, it can be extremely frightening. By developing good stepladders with small steps, you can reduce the fear. But it isn't possible to get rid of it entirely. Your child is going to have to face fear to overcome fear.

We all need encouragement to help us to do unpleasant or difficult things. As an adult, you can recognize the value of unpleasant things. For example, if you have to undergo a painful operation, you would do it because you realize it will help you in the long run. But children are not as good at recognizing what is good for them. One of the biggest differences between adults and children is that children have very little understanding of the future and the concept of time. Telling children, "You have to go through this pain now because it will be good for you later," just doesn't make the same sense to them as it generally does to adults.

For this reason, one of the really important parts of reality testing is to give your child rewards when he or she successfully completes a step. Giving rewards after each practice increases your child's motivation because it balances the unpleasantness of reality testing with a positive experience.

Over the years, we have occasionally come across some parents who do not feel that they should reward their child for doing reality testing exercises. After all, other kids can do these things without problems, so why should your child be rewarded for doing something that other kids do easily? The point is that all children are different. For whatever reason, your child doesn't find these things easy, even though other children might. To put it in context, imagine forcing yourself to sing a song on national television or to climb into a cage full of poisonous snakes. The level of fear you might feel doing these things is no more than what you are asking your own child to face. It's necessary for your child to do these things so that he or she learns to overcome his or her fears, but it won't be easy. Offering rewards for his or her attempts is the only way you will motivate your child to try these things, and it will also communicate to your child your pride at what she or he is doing. A reward is not a bribe. Bribes are things you give someone to make them do something that is of benefit to you. A reward is simply a motivator to encourage your child to do something that will ultimately benefit him or her. A reward is also a signal of your pride and approval in your child's behavior.

We have covered all of the important facts about how to give rewards in chapter 5, so we won't go through it again here. We urge you to reread that section in order to remind yourself of the important points. We have listed some of the main points to remember:

- Rewards do not have to be financial, but can also include fun activities.

- Rewards do not have to be large, but simply need to be relevant to your child.

- The reward should be an appropriate size for the difficulty of the step.

- Rewards need to be given as soon as possible after your child has done what he or she agreed.

- You need to be consistent—give the reward if your child has earned it, but don't give it if the step hasn't been done.

- Reward your child for doing the step whether or not he or she was scared.

Step 5: Doing Reality Testing

At this point, you and your child should have brainstormed a series of situations that your child is frightened of, organized these situations into one or more stepladders, and decided on a few rewards for the first few steps of the stepladders. Your child is now ready to begin facing his or her fears.

To begin reality testing, your child should pick the first step of one or two stepladders. You and your child may want to set a date and time that he or she will try it. It's also possible to leave it up to your child more. For example, you may simply decide that he or she needs to do the first step "some time this week." How specific you are will depend on the age of your child, the type of step, and what point you are up to in the program. Generally, early on in the program it is a good idea to be more specific and actually set a date and time for practice. This is especially important with younger children. However, it will depend on the type of step. Some steps can be done when it suits you (e.g. calling for information on the telephone) while others will depend on the task (e.g. answering the telephone when it rings). Don't forget to reward children when they've done their practice.

To help your child get the most out of his or her practice, we have included the following form, called "Fighting Fear by Facing Fear." Your child should keep a record of all his or her practice. This helps to make sure the practice is done and to let you know when practice is slowing down. It will also provide a great record of achievements that your child can look back on when his or her motivation begins to drop. The form also encourages your child to think about what strategies he or she used.

Fighting Fear by Facing Fear

What did I do? _____

_____

Worry Scale   Before _____   After _____

What reward did I get? _____

What did I learn? _____

_____

What did I do? _____

_____

Worry Scale   Before _____   After _____

What reward did I get? _____

What did I learn? _____

_____

What did I do? _____

_____

Worry Scale   Before _____   After _____

What reward did I get? _____

What did I learn? _____

_____

Keep Going

Encourage your child to keep going with the program even when the going gets tough. Just like learning anything new, the more they practice, the easier it will become.

Children need to practice the same step several times until they are confident trying it, even to the point where they may say it's boring or they never had a problem with it anyway. Repeating the reality testing steps strengthens children's learning of new ways of doing things by giving them more success and a growing feeling of mastery over the fear. Your child has probably had many experiences of feeling "a failure." Trying the reality testing steps several times proves to children that they can do it, and it's essential to overcome these well-established expectations.

Where there are difficulties or things do not go well at the first attempt, this too is a valuable opportunity to encourage your child to persist, to learn that a "failure" is not a disaster and to look at how he or she may want to do it differently next time.

Adding New Step-by-Step Plans

As your child progresses up the first ladder, you may think about starting on another of his or her stepladders. Children can usually work on two or three different stepladders at the same time.

As your child gains more confidence and becomes used to the ideas of reality testing, you and your child will come across opportunities for what we call "spontaneous practice." Spontaneous practice refers to opportunities to practice facing fears that were not actually part of your child's stepladder, but have just come up in your child's daily life. For example, if your child is shy and has a fear of meeting new people, you may be sitting in a park one day and notice another child shooting a basketball by him or herself. Although this specific situation may not be on your child's stepladder, you should encourage your child to grab the opportunity to join the other child as a way of facing the fear of meeting a new person. In some cases, these opportunities may even be a few steps higher than your child is currently at on his or her stepladder. If your child is willing to have a go, he or she should be encouraged and rewarded.

Other Resources

Use resources in the community, family, and school system to provide a wide range of reality testing situations. Most people are willing to assist children who are learning new skills and readily understand the basic concepts involved once they are explained. Encourage grandparents and others not to be too helpful and to allow the child to experience some anxiety to overcome the fears.

Class teachers or school counselors may be useful in helping to discreetly organize reality-testing steps in real-life settings at school. From our experience, they are very open to involvement in these programs.

Summarizing the Steps of Reality Testing

The process of conducting an effective reality testing program involves being realistic, responsive, and repetitive and rewarding application and success.

- Choose *realistic* goals: Choose goals that can be achieved and are appropriate to your child's developmental level and capabilities. The shy child will probably never become the Mr. or Ms. Personality of the class, but he or she can aim to be able to speak up in class, give a talk, call friends to ask them over, and be able to speak to the school principal.

  Your child does not have to be totally free of anxiety. A certain amount of anxiety is normal and realistic in certain situations and may even be performance enhancing. This program focuses on reducing excessive anxiety. Your child needs to learn that she or he can tolerate a certain level of anxiety and to go ahead and "just do it."

- Respond by adjusting the program if difficulties occur: You need to monitor your child's progress and adjust the steps in response to the progress being made. It may be necessary to slip in new items to bridge a gap between the steps, if there is reluctance to move to the next one. Sometimes the step can be altered by adding different people present or varying the place the task is to be performed. Moving through the items too quickly may mean the steps are not difficult enough. It may also be a form of avoidance as questioning can reveal that the child has not stayed in the situation long enough.

- Repetition is the key to long term results: It is important to remember that the best results and most long lasting benefits from the program will come from lots of practice and repeating steps over and over until your child feels confident in doing it. Look for a feeling of "I don't need to practice that, it doesn't really bother me anymore."

- *Reward* effort and success: Maintain the reward program consistently throughout the reality-testing process. Encourage children to reward themselves both for achieving a step and for their efforts in trying hard. You should keep up the praise and the rewards. Anxious children need reinforcement of their efforts to encourage them to keep going in the face of frustration.

Good intentions to reward children for progress can be easily overlooked after some progress. However, the reward program and parental praise should be continued right through the steps of reality testing.

Dealing with Difficulties

Reality testing is the most important component of this program to help your child overcome his or her fears. However, there are many ways in which reality testing can go wrong. We don't mean that you can harm your child. Rather, there are some ways of doing reality testing that are really effective and other ways that may be less effective. In the rest of this chapter, we will discuss some of the problems you might come across with your child's reality testing and some ways of overcoming these problems.

Getting Stuck

With the gains they are making, regular praise from parents and others, and the chance to earn rewards, most children enjoy reality testing and make rapid gains. However, some children may find the going tough, and things may not go as smoothly as you would like. Children may get stuck on a step and refuse to try the next one, may move through the steps very slowly, or may want to give up the reality testing altogether. If this is the case for your child, there are several things you can try.

First, summarize the progress that your child has made so far by repeating the last few steps that he or she has successfully done. Use this opportunity to really praise your child for their efforts and the gains that they have made. You may need to repeat this process several times to build up children's confidence in their capacity to face their fears.

Next, revise the thinking realistically skills in relation to the new step. In particular, look carefully for any underlying worries your child may have. There may be unforeseen worries that your child has not admitted before that need to be dealt with before your child can move on.

Third, brainstorm ways in which the next step can be broken down into slightly smaller steps. This is especially important if your child has been moving along well and all of a sudden has become stuck. In this case, it's very possible that the next step is just too big a jump.

You also need to think about your own role in the process. You need to think about your own attitudes and feelings toward your child's progress. Anxious children can be very sensitive to their parent's concerns. If you personally are worried about the next step or are not totally convinced about the value of reality testing, you may inadvertently be giving your child subtle messages that are interfering with his or her progress.

You also need to ask yourself whether you have been holding up your end of the bargain. Have you been rewarding your child as promised? Have the rewards been consistently delivered? Have they been given immediately? Have you been praising your child and putting effort into the program? You need to be very honest with yourself about the answers to these questions. If you are not consistent and do not support and reward your child as promised, you cannot expect him or her to take the program seriously.

Finally, you need to ask yourself whether you might have some worries about how much to push your child to try something a bit harder. Often there may be a "soft" and a "hard" parent, and disagreement between you as parents or one parent opting out of the treatment plan can reduce your child's enthusiasm. Try to talk these issues over and agree on a joint strategy to help your child. If you are finding it hard to "be tough" and push your child, you may need to try some of the realistic thinking on your own worries. As long as you continue to show your child that you love him or her, pushing your child will not cause them to hate you or to become mentally scarred or damaged. Remember that being a little tough now will help your child become more confident in the long run.

Need for Reassurance

We discussed the issue of reassurance-seeking in the chapter on child management (chapter 5). While seeking excessive reassurance can be a problem in many areas of an anxious child's life, it may become especially apparent during reality testing.

When you do reality testing, you may find that your child constantly asks questions such as, "What is going to happen?" "Exactly what time will you be back?" or "Will you be okay?" Being a loving parent, it can be very hard to ignore these requests. But it's important not to give in and provide too much reassurance for your child during reality testing. This does not mean that you need to be nasty or hard, but rather that you gradually need to encourage your child to rely more and more on his or her own judgment. If seeking reassurance is a particular problem for your child, you may need to try and include it into the stepladder. For example, you may encourage your child to sleep at a friend's house as one step and allow some reassurance questions, then the next step might repeat the process but without allowing any questioning. You may want to go back to chapter 5 to reread the section on dealing with reassurance.

Lashi's Example

Lashi had been working on one of her stepladders for going to sleep in her own bed with the light off. She was doing very well and was finally able to sleep in her own bed all night and was allowing her mother to turn off all the lights in her part of the house. But there was still an anxious habit that needed to be addressed. Every night when Lashi went to bed, she would call her mother to her room four or five times before she finally went to sleep. At these times, Lashi would ask a bunch of questions such as, "Are you staying home tonight?" "Have you checked the doors and windows?" and "How long will you be up?" Lashi's mother was answering all these questions because she was so pleased with Lashi's progress. But she soon realized that she was going to have to work on this reassurance-seeking, because it was stopping Lashi from becoming self-confident. Lashi and her mother discussed how they could include these questions into Lashi's stepladder. At first, Lashi could call her mother into her room twice before she went to sleep. After that, her mother would ignore her. At the next step, Lashi could only call her mother into her room once after going to bed. Then Lashi and her mother would go through Lashi's realistic thinking before Lashi went to bed, but she could not call her mother after going to bed. Finally, Lashi was rewarded only for going to bed without any reassurance from her mother either before or after going to bed.

Dealing with "Failure"

Anxious children seem to have more sensitive "failure" detectors than other children, so the importance of a minor setback in doing a simple task will be greatly magnified in their eyes. This can be a blow to their confidence and result in an increased level of anxiety about attempting any further items or even about doing things they found quite easy before. Many anxious children easily slip into negative self-talk such as "I'm hopeless. I knew I couldn't do anything right."

If your child tries one of his or her steps and suddenly finds that it's too hard or is not able to do it all as planned, he or she may see this as a complete failure. If this happens, it's important to encourage children to do their realistic thinking about the importance of the success or failure of their efforts. Role reversal is a particularly good source of evidence to use. In other words, ask children to imagine what they would say to someone else who was in the same position. Try to point out that there is no real failure in doing reality testing. Each attempt is an opportunity to learn. If they were not able to do that step, it simply means that the step was too hard and they need to break it down into smaller, easier steps.

On the other side of the coin, some anxious children actually get worried about being successful because then they might have to do even better next time. In other words, for some kids, doing a good job makes them feel under more pressure for the next time. If this is true for your child, you may find that he or she downplays or even completely denies his or her successes. This tends to happen particularly in very perfectionistic children.

You will need to stress to your child that doing reality testing is what counts—not winning or being the best. Again, remind them that there is no way to fail reality testing—they just need to do it. You may also want to include some reality testing exercises aimed at reducing any perfectionism.

Taking On Too Much

A different sort of problem that you may come across happens if your child is trying really hard to please you and be the "perfect child." In this case, you may find that your child will choose steps for reality testing that are just too hard. Sometimes, it's also easy for you to get caught up in the excitement and begin to encourage your child to take on harder and harder steps and you might begin to go a bit too quickly.

It's important to praise your child for his or her enthusiasm. Having a child who wants to try hard is wonderful. But you also need to remind your child that everyone is individual and that there are no prizes for being the first to finish. If the steps are too big, your child is more likely not to be able to do them and may then begin to lose confidence. Go back to the list and make sure that the big steps are broken down into more manageable and easier steps.

Speeding Through

In some cases, children can have a sort of "breakthrough." In other words, by facing one or two situations that they may have avoided for years, they get a sudden burst of confidence and lose their fears very quickly. If this happens, it can be wonderful.

However, for other children, moving too quickly through the steps may be a sign that they're not learning anything from the reality testing. On the one hand, it may mean that the steps are just not challenging enough for your child. If this is the case, you'll need to sit down together and come up with some more difficult steps. On the other hand, the steps may be so difficult that your child is not willing to stay in the situation long enough for him or her to learn that nothing bad will happen. Or it may be that your child is "cheating" a little and not fully engaging in each step. If this is the case, you simply need to encourage your child to redo the steps, but include more detail in the instructions you give. For example, you may need to specify how long your child stays in the situation or you may instruct him or her in such things as where to sit and how much he or she has to say.

George's Example

One of George's big fears was going to parties and having to mix socially with other kids. After doing reality testing for a while and gradually building his confidence, an opportunity came up when he was invited to a party at a friend's house. Even though this was pretty scary for George, his parents encouraged him to put it on his stepladder and have a go. When George came home after the party, his father asked him how it went. "Fine," was all he said. Something in his tone made his father think that it all seemed too easy. So he asked George to sit down and tell him exactly what he had done at the party. George looked sheepish and admitted that he had gone to the party as they agreed, but he'd spent the entire evening sitting in a corner watching everyone. George got his reward as agreed for going to the party, but his parents suggested that next time he would need to make sure he mixed with some of the kids. When the next party came up, the step was not only to go to the party, but to make sure that George spoke with at least three different kids while there. This time when he got home, George said that it had been pretty hard but he was also surprised at how much he had in common with one kid there and they actually got on quite well.

Ups and Downs

During the reality testing process there will be some days that seem better than others, and progress will not always be smooth. You should act as a coach to encourage children to do the best they can on any given day and to keep trying the next day. On bad days it may be better to repeat a step already achieved rather than try a new, more difficult step. Rewarding good attempts by your child, in addition to rewarding success at achieving the step, will foster your child's ability to persist and to tolerate what he or she perceives as failure.

Worried Sick

Most parents and therapists would agree that anxious children and adolescents "wrote the book" when it comes to excuses and explanations about why they can't do something.

A common, and sometimes extremely difficult, problem for parents to deal with is complaints of illness at times of stress. Headaches, upset stomachs, and generally "feeling sick" are difficult to deal with when you're not sure of the cause. Sometimes parents or grandparents have different views about the reason for the complaints.

Consultation with the family doctor may be necessary to exclude physical problems as a first step. This is important if there is disagreement between you and your child's other primary caregiver over the cause of the complaints and the most appropriate way to manage them. It's important that there is a consistent approach by everyone involved. In families where the parents are divorced and the child moves between two households, these issues will need the involvement and agreement of all the adults involved in the child's care. This can include the school teacher and school nurse.

This is especially important in families with a history of physical illness where there may be real anxieties about physical pain that need to be dealt with first. If this applies to your family, you may need to work through your concerns about this issue. Try to use realistic thinking about your own concerns about your child's health. Look at the realistic consequences of both encouraging your child to challenge his or her fears and of allowing the avoidance to continue and perhaps worsen.

Lashi's Example

As they moved through the program, Lashi's mother decided that it was time that she started to go out and leave Lashi at home with a sitter. On the first night that she was getting ready to go out, Lashi began to cry and throw a huge tantrum. She became so worked up that she vomited. Lashi's mother ended up canceling the sitter and staying home. After that, Lashi began to complain of stomachaches and feeling sick every time her mother wanted to go anywhere and even on some days when she had to go to school. Sometimes, Lashi got so worked up that she would make herself physically sick.

As a first step, Lashi's mother took her to the doctor to get a full checkup. "All clear" was the doctor's diagnosis. "This is a healthy little girl." After that, Lashi's mother told her that when they worked on the stepladder, they would do whatever they had agreed to whether or not Lashi felt sick. Lashi's mother contacted the school and they agreed that if Lashi felt sick at school, she could go to the nurse and rest for a while and then she would go back to class— Lashi's mother would not come and pick her up unless she had a fever.

Soon after, Lashi's mother was asked to a party. Lashi and her mother discussed the situation and decided that this was a reasonable step for the stepladder. However, on the night of the party, Lashi began to feel sick and have pains. Lashi's mother told her that she understood how hard it all was and that she really felt bad about her pain, but that she was going to go to the party anyway. She gave the sitter detailed instructions about how to handle Lashi and to call her only if Lashi had a fever. That night was hard for both Lashi and her mom but in the morning Lashi got a big reward for doing her step from the stepladder. Lashi's mom went out on two more occasions with the same results. It was not easy, but they both stuck with it.

Finally, on the fourth time, Lashi was not sick when her mom went out. Even though she was still scared, she did not throw up and did not complain of stomachaches. To celebrate, Lashi got an extra reward the next morning.

Smart Tricks

People can reduce their fear by superstitions and idiosyncratic behaviors such as carrying a lucky charm or special toy, wearing certain lucky clothes, humming a song, chewing gum, or going through a particular ritual before doing something that causes anxiety. All these methods of avoidance are used by adults, including sports stars and actors, and they are often used by anxious children.

These beliefs and behaviors can act as subtle ways of avoiding facing up to the feared situation. If children use any of these subtle types of avoidance, the big risk is that they may not believe that his or her success is due to their own ability. Instead, he or she may attribute success to the special object.

To properly overcome anxiety, your child needs to experience the fear, use the realistic thinking techniques to realistically assess the level of danger, and then experience the situation to learn that there was no need for that level of concern. Your child must be able to attribute their lack of fear to a *real* lack of danger, not to the magic protective powers of a lucky charm, crystal, or special socks.

Children with separation fears are increasingly reliant upon having instant access to their parents, because of the mobile cell phone, and this is a type of subtle avoidance. You may find that your own anxieties can play a part in this overreliance on immediate contact as well. Look carefully at the line between safety issues and the convenience of being in reasonable contact with each other and a subtle avoidance of dealing with fears about separation.

A special example of subtle avoidance might be found in children who are taking medication for their anxiety. If your child is on antianxiety medication while doing reality testing, it is very possible that he or she will think, "The only reason I could do that was because my medication helped me through it." In this case, your child will not be building his or her own confidence, but instead will be learning that he or she can only cope with the help of a drug.

The existence of lucky charms, aids, or medication is not a major problem. It simply means that the reality testing steps will need to be repeated at some point without the special object. In the case of charms or other aids, you can actually organize the steps so that they are each done the first time with the aid and then repeated without it. In the case of medication, your child may need to complete all or most of his or her anxiety program while taking the medication. Then, when improvements seem to be going very well, you may want to begin to reduce the medication under the guidance of the prescribing physician. Once the medication has been stopped, you will need to go through a few of the reality testing steps again, just to convince your child that it really is him or her who is in control.

Talia's Example

Talia had been working on her stepladder of going swimming for some time and was getting really confident in the water. Talia's dad really wanted to be involved and had taken an active part in the whole process. As part of his involvement, Talia's father had been going with her through all of the steps of her stepladder. Each time Talia went into the water, her dad would stand outside and watch her. Talia regularly waved to her dad and would look at him a lot. On one occasion, Talia was at the beach swimming and having a great time. Her dad decided to go off to get an ice cream. When he returned, Talia was out of the water and crying. She screamed at him, "Where did you go—I might have drowned." Talia's father suddenly realized that by being with her for all of her steps, Talia had learned to use him as a safety cue. As a result, Talia could only face deep water when he was around. Talia and her dad discussed the problem and decided that she needed to start over and redo most of her stepladder, but this time without her dad being there. Going through the stepladder the second time was much faster and it wasn't long before Talia's confidence in the water was sky-high.

In Summary

When teaching children how to overcome their fears with reality testing, the following points should be covered:

- Reality testing is a step-by-step process to test out the reality of a child's fears. The fears are faced gradually, working from least feared to the most feared situations.

- Goals should be realistic, within the child's capacities, and appropriate to his or her age.

- Repeating the steps and constant practice establish the new skill and promote confidence and mastery in the child.

- Rewards are an important component to enhance motivation, reinforce the child's attempts, encourage persistence, and acknowledge success and effort.

- Respond to difficulties and setbacks by adjusting the reality testing hierarchy. Remember that "failure" is merely another opportunity to learn.

Chapter 7

Social Skills and Assertiveness

In this chapter you will learn:

- to understand the importance of social skills and assertiveness

- to understand which social skills children need to learn

- to teach your child some of the most essential social skills

- to encourage your child to practice his or her social skills in social situations

- to create opportunities in which your child can use his or her new skills

George spends most of his spare time alone. Even at school you'll find him on his own. He rarely speaks to his classmates. At lunchtime, he usually goes to the library and sits on his own reading a book. Sometimes he walks around the school and stops to watch some of his classmates playing soccer. They never ask him to join in. In fact, they don't notice that he's there. George would love to join in, but he can't think of how to ask, and he's afraid that they will laugh at him or refuse to let him play. He returns to the classroom after lunch and sits at the back of the class hoping not to be called upon to answer any questions. He doesn't speak to the other students. He really likes the girl who sits in front of him in science class. He would love to talk to her, he can't think of what to say and is afraid that he would get it wrong and feel stupid. The teacher is going around the class asking each student to give an idea for the school festival. George thinks it would be a good idea to run a coconut stall where you win a prize for knocking the coconut off a stand. George's turn comes. He looks down at his desk and mumbles, wishing that he could disappear. He tries to explain his idea to the teacher, but his voice is too quiet and no one can hear him. The teacher moves on to the next person in the class.

After school, George walks home on his own. One of his classmates goes the same way home. George notices that the boy has dropped his school folder and the pages are flying around. George wants to offer to help, but is not sure what to say. He walks past, leaving the boy to pick up the papers on his own.

The next day, George is standing in line in the cafeteria, waiting to buy some lunch. Another boy pushes in front of George, leaving George feeling angry. He would love to tell the boy to go to the back of the end of the line, but he doesn't say anything.

Why Are Social Skills and Assertiveness Important?

Children need to be successful in a wide range of situations with other children and with adults, including parents and teachers. For example, with other children they need to be able to hold conversations, ask to join in games or activities, and invite other children to play or to come over for a visit. They need to be able to ask questions, ask to have a turn in a game, give compliments, offer toys or items to other children, and assert their rights if they're unfairly treated. All these activities are important if children are to make friends and be accepted into their peer group.

Children also need to be able to handle adults. For example, they need to be able to ask for help when they need it, offer to help, express their point of view, pick the right moment to interrupt, answer questions, and start and maintain conversations with adults. When you start to think about it, there are an enormous number of social tasks that children have to be able to perform in a competent way. By the time children reach adolescence, there are an even greater number of social situations that they have to learn to handle, including romantic relationships, getting through job interviews and keeping a job.

The skills that we need to perform these social tasks success-fully are called *social skills*. Our research shows that some anxious children perform more poorly than other children on many social tasks. There are two possibilities why this might be the case. It might be that some anxious children are too afraid to use their skills. Alter-natively, some anxious children may not develop their social skills because they have less experience and practice at interacting with other children. Many anxious children avoid interactions with others and therefore may have less opportunity to practice how to interact with other people. Whatever the explanation, our research has shown that there are significant benefits to teaching anxious children social skills in order to improve their relationships with others. Anx-ious children tend also not to be very assertive. *Assertiveness* is the ability to express your needs, to assert your rights with other people, and to stick up for yourself in a way that produces a positive outcome.

This chapter will focus on ways that you can help your child manage some of the difficult social situations of everyday life. We will cover four main areas of social skills:

- body language skills (eye contact, posture, facial expression)
- voice quality skills (tone and pitch, volume, rate, and clarity)
- conversation skills (greetings, introductions, starting and holding conversations)
- friendship skills (giving compliments, offering help, offering invi-tations, asking to join in)
- assertiveness skills (asking for help, saying "no," dealing with teasing or bullying)

Not all children have problems in all of these areas. Below, we have provided a list of some of the most important skills. We have put the following skills into a table so that the information is easy to follow. Read through this table and then observe children carefully over the next few days. Decide whether you think that they're performing well for each of these social skills, and write down if you think that they need to work on any of these areas. Their performance does not need to be perfect, but make a note if you think their poor perform-ance of a particular skill is causing problems in their relationships with others. Remember that the social skills that children and adoles-cents use are different from the ones that we use as adults. In observ-ing your child, try not to look at them from an adult perspective, but think about whether their skills seem comparable to those of other kids their age.

Area	Specific Skill	Description of Skill	Check Here If Your Child Has a Problem with This Skill
Body language	Eye contact	Child looks others in the eye during conversations to show that he or she is listening and paying attention, but does not stare excessively. Many anxious children avoid making eye contact and tend to look down or away when talking to others. This may be seen by others as indicating unfriendliness and lack of interest. It's also a problem if children make too much eye contact during conversations and stare at others too much, as this makes other people feel uncomfortable.	
	Posture	Child sits or stands in a way that's appropriate for the situation. Some postures, may create a poor impression upon others. (e.g. slumped, hunched up, turning away from the other person, or excessively rigid and upright.)	

	Facial expression	Child's facial expressions are appropriate to the situation. Smiles and has a friendly face when talking generally with others. Uses sad and angry facial expressions occasionally, appropriate to the situation.	
		Facial expressions communicate how we're feeling. Bored, angry, or fearful facial expressions or lack of smiling may be seen by other children and adults as a sign of unfriendliness.	
Voice quality	Tone and pitch	Child's speech is usually friendly, pleasant to listen to, and expressive. The child can use different tones of voice to communicate different emotions.	
		If a child's voice sounds boring, aggressive, fearful, or whining, or is unpleasant to listen to, then this may lead to misunderstandings with other people. Other people may misinterpret the child as being unfriendly, aggressive, or uninterested. Children need to be able to use a friendly tone of voice in most situations.	
	Volume	Child's volume of speech is appropriate for different situations.	

	Volume	Children need to be able to speak up so that they're heard, and yet not to speak so loud as to be inappropriate. Many anxious children speak too quietly, which interferes with their communication with others.	
	Rate	Child speaks at an appropriate rate—not too fast and not too slow. Very slow speech may sound boring. Very fast speech is hard to follow.	
	Clarity	Child speaks clearly and is easy to understand. Conversations are difficult if children's speech is hard to follow. Some anxious children tend to mumble and have difficulty speaking clearly so that others can understand them.	
Conversation skills	Greetings and introductions	Child says "hello" or other greeting when meeting people he or she knows. For older children, the ability to introduce themselves to others is especially important. Most children know what to say when they greet someone, but they may be too anxious to do so or they may not do so in a socially skilled way. In all conversation skills, children must remember to use the basic skills of eye contact, appropriate facial expression, and clear, audible speech.	

	Starting conversations	Child is able to start a conversation by asking simple questions or making simple statements. Some anxious children avoid starting conversations with others. They tend to be quiet most of the time, particularly with people that they don't know well. This makes it difficult for them to form friendships with other children.	
	Holding conversations: answering questions	Child listens to what the other person has said and answers with some detail, rather than very brief answers. Some anxious children give very short answers when other people ask them a question. The information that they give is minimal and does not convey the message that he or she would like to continue the conversation.	
	Holding conversations: asking questions	Child asks appropriate questions to the other person to allow the conversation to continue. The questions are likely to be of interest to the other person. Children need to be able to ask questions in order to continue a conversation. Children talk about a wide range of topics.	

	Holding conversations: taking turns	Child takes turns in conversations, listening to others and then returning with an appropriate comment or question. Two-way conversation skills are important if children are going to form friendships. Some anxious children have difficulties in holding conversations. Their responses to questions tend to be very short, and they rarely ask questions or make statements back to the other person voluntarily. This can be misinterpreted as an indication that the child is not interested and does not wish to be friendly. It also makes it hard for other children to get to know them.	
	Choosing topics of conversation	Child picks appropriate topics of conversation. It's important that children can pick conversation topics that the other person is interested in and that are appropriate to the situation. Anxious children often have difficulty thinking of things to talk about. They need to learn about the types of things that other children are interested in if they're going to form friendships.	
	Uses polite conversation	Child uses polite speech and says please and thank you as appropriate.	

	Uses polite conver-sation	For most children this is not a problem, but we mention it because the rules of polite communication are important in determining the impression that children make upon adults (e.g. teachers) and peers.	
Friend-ship skills	Offering help or items	Child offers to help other children or adults, or offers to lend or give items where appropriate. Forming friendships requires that children can show kind-ness to others. One part of this is to be able to offer to help others when they need it. Friendship involves reciprocity in giving and receiving help of various kinds. Some anxious children will stand by and do nothing when they really want to help. This may then be misinterpreted as unfriendliness and lack of caring.	
	Offering invitations	Child invites other children to join in with activities or offers invitations to come over to his or her house (or other similar activity). Friendships involve spending time together and making an effort by showing that you would like to make friends. Offering invitations to others and initiating activities is part of this process.	

	Asking to join in	Child will approach other children to ask to join in his or her activity. Many anxious children are reluctant to ask other children if they can join in their activity. Often they really want to join in, but they stand on the edge of the activity watching. They may not know what to say or may be too afraid to try for fear of looking foolish.	
	Expressing affection	Child expresses affection toward children and adults where appropriate, either using speech or physical gestures (e.g. holds hands, hugs, touches gently, pats on the back). The ability to show affection is important in forming friendships with peers. This may be something very simple and physical and does not have to be verbal.	
	Giving compliments	Child gives compliments to others (adults and children) when appropriate. The ability to give positive feedback to other people is an important part of friendship. It shows that one is interested in the other person and wants to make them feel good. This is just as important in children's friendships as it is in adult relationships.	

	Shows caring when others are hurt or upset	Child tries to help others and to care for them when they are hurt or upset. Children need to be sensitive to other people and to show that they care when others are hurt or upset. Children cannot always do something to help, but they can try to check that the other person is okay, and try to comfort them in some way. This may be physical (e.g. a gentle touch, a spoken comment, or asking someone else to help).	
Assertiveness	Sticking up for one's rights	Child is able to stick up for his or her rights without causing harm to other people. There are many situations in which children have to learn how to stick up for themselves. There will be times when other children or adults try to take advantage of them, do not attend to their needs, or pressure them into doing something that they don't want to do. In all instances, it's important that children deal with these situations in a way that does not cause harm to other people. If children are too active in asserting themselves, then this may become aggression. Very anxious children tend to be unassertive and have difficulty sticking up for their rights.	

	Sticking up for one's rights	Assertiveness requires communication of clear messages, in a loud, strong voice (not aggressive). It requires being able to say how one feels and exactly what one does or does not want to happen. If the problem is too difficult to solve, the child may need to actively seek help from an adult.	
	Asking for help or information or expressing needs	Child is able to ask for help or information and to inform others when he or she needs something. It's particularly important at school that children can ask for help, clarification, or information from their teachers when they need it. Problems may arise if children remain silent when they are in need of help. Children also need to be able to request help from their peers.	
	Saying no	Child is able to refuse unreasonable requests and to say no when he or she wishes to do so.	

	Saying no	It's important that children are able to say when they don't want to do something. They need to be able to say how they feel and to refuse unreasonable requests from others. Some children may find themselves doing things that they don't want to do or having things taken from them because they did not clearly state how they felt and did not clearly communicate the answer "no."	
	Dealing with teasing	Child is able to deal successfully with teasing from others. All children have to deal with teasing. They need to be able to put a stop to excessive teasing and to learn not to become too hurt by it. Of course, if it's very frequent and severe, you and your school may need to become involved.	
	Dealing with bullying	Child is able to address bullying from others, either using their own strategies or by seeking the help of others.	

Dealing with bullying	As with teasing, all children have to deal with incidents of bullying at some point in their lives. However, no child should have to put up with bullying, and we will discuss various ways in which it can be stopped. Children need to be able to put a stop to bullying, and there are various ways of handling it. Again, parents and schools need to become involved in ongoing cases.	

Teaching Social Skills

There are many in ways in which you can teach social skills to your child. The strategies that you use for teaching will depend upon how much difficulty your child has in using social skills. Some children have just a few areas of difficulty. Others may have poor performance on many of the skills described in the table we provided. For those children who have just a few areas of difficulty, we use a strategy called incidental teaching.

Incidental Teaching

Incidental teaching involves using opportunities that occur in everyday life to teach a particular skill, rather than having special teaching sessions that are dedicated to training your child to use social skills. Incidental teaching involves:

- identifying social situations in which particular social skills are needed

- explaining to your child that a particular skill is needed in that situation and how it should be performed

- explaining why it is important

- checking that your child has understood what is needed

- prompting your child to use the skill

- praising your child for attempting to use the skill and telling them what he or she did well

- giving your child gentle feedback about ways in which the skill could be improved

When you are using incidental teaching, it's important that you keep things really simple and stick to one skill at a time. Children become confused if they have to concentrate on too many things at once. When an appropriate situation arises, decide which skill is most important. Make sure that the skill is not too difficult and that your child has learned more simple skills first.

For example, George's parents noticed that he rarely made eye contact with other children or with his teachers when they spoke to him. George tended to look down or away when other people talked to him. George and his father had to attend a parent-teacher evening at the school. His father suggested that George work on making eye contact with his teacher during the interview. George and his father discussed why it was important to make eye contact and how this influenced the impression that people make upon each other. George understood what was required and laughed when he found himself making eye contact with his father. Just prior to going into the classroom for their interview, George's father prompted his son to remind him to use eye contact with the teacher. During the interview George tried hard and his father noticed George making occasional eye contact with the teacher. Once they were alone again, his father told George how well he had done and how he had noticed the big improvement. They talked about how it had felt and about other situations in which eye contact would be important.

Helping Children Who Need More Intensive Teaching

Some children will need more intensive teaching in order to learn to be more socially skilled. Here are some guidelines about how to teach social skills to your child using a more structured approach. The teaching methods are basically the same as for incidental teaching. For each skill you will be using the following methods to teach the skill:

- instructions and explanation

- practice of the skill, and prompting

- feedback

- praise

Social skills are like building blocks. Often it's difficult to know which skills to teach and where to start. We believe that children need to work on each small skill and then gradually put them all together to create a good performance. We suggest that you start with body language skills and then move on to conversation skills when your child is proficient at those skills.

When you're teaching social skills to your child, he or she may feel a bit uncomfortable and embarrassed. It's helpful to use games and enjoyable activities when you're teaching social skills. Humor is also a good way of reducing anxiety and making the sessions enjoyable. However, it is important to laugh *with* your child and not *at* your child.

Giving Instructions

When you teach a skill to a child, you need to begin by giving information about the skill. In particular, you need to give information about:

- Exactly what is involved in the skill? How is it performed?

- Why is it important? What happens if the skill is not used?

Having discussed the skill, it's important then to demonstrate how the skill is performed. Begin with a description of the skill to be taught. Ideally you should focus on just one skill at a time, and that becomes the theme of the session. You can regard yourself a bit like a coach in a sport situation. Having described the skill to be learned, you need to demonstrate exactly how the skill is used. You can demonstrate it yourself or find some real-life examples to watch. You can watch other people in a shopping center or on television and discuss how they're using the skill.

It's often interesting to demonstrate what happens when the skill is not used. This can produce some funny situations. For example, you can pretend to hold a conversation with your child without using any eye contact. You can then discuss why eye contact is important. When you are watching TV together, you can look for people who do not use the skill well. One good idea, especially with younger children, is to watch their favorite television show together and see who can pick examples of good and bad skills quickest.

The instructions phase is more difficult with younger children, basically consisting of giving prompts or requests for use of the skill. For example, "Paul, I'm going to ask you a question and when you give your answer, I want you to use a loud, clear voice so that I can hear what you say. Can we try that now?" With younger children, you can also demonstrate skills using puppets. For example, two puppets can demonstrate how to say "hello" and ask questions of each other. You can also use puppets to demonstrate use of appropriate eye contact and voice volume.

Pointing out that children who do not use social skills very well tend to be less popular and that learning to use these skills well will help in making friends may help to motivate your child.

Practicing Body Language and Conversation Skills

Once you've explained to your child how a skill should be performed, it's time to start to practice using the skill. To begin with, it is best to practice in the safety of your home, where things can't go too wrong. In the same way that you need to practice hitting a tennis ball in order to become a proficient tennis player, progress in social skills will only be made with regular practice. Ideally, your child should practice every day.

In the teaching of the more simple social skills, such as body language or conversation skills, we suggest that you use practice cue cards. Topics are written onto the cue cards and used to trigger conversations in which each skill can be practiced. Try to think of topics of conversation that you could practice with your child. These cue cards are used to enable your child to practice the particular skill that you are working on. For example, one time you might use the cue cards to work on eye contact. On a different occasion you might focus on increasing voice volume.

Here are some examples of cue cards that you might find useful:

• What is your favorite movie? Now tell me what the film was about.

• What is your favorite book? Now tell me all about the story in the book.

• Tell me about your favorite hobby.

- Pick someone in your family. What exactly does this person look like?
- Tell me about what you did last weekend.
- What is your favorite TV show? Explain to me why you like it.
- Ask me some questions about when I was a child.
- Ask me about what I did last weekend.
- Ask me about people in my family.
- Ask me about where I would like to go for a holiday.

When you're teaching a new skill, it's important to stick to one skill at a time. Only move on to teaching the next skill once your child is able to perform the first one reasonably well. When you move on to a new skill, you need to keep prompting your child to remember to use the body language and voice skills that they've already learned. For example, when you're teaching your child to ask questions, here are some prompts you can give your child: "Pick a sensible topic, make clear eye contact, use a friendly facial expression, and ask your question in a clear, loud voice." Also, you will need to spend some time talking about how to choose appropriate topics for starting up a conversation. For example, topics might concern a TV program, a sports team, the local news, movies, pets, hobbies, or asking about other people (e.g. their health, their opinion, their favorite activity). Together with your child you might like to make a list of topics that children at school tend to talk about in their free time.

When your child has learned the basics of body language and conversation skills, you can move on to teach more complicated social skills relating to making friends and assertiveness. In addition to the teaching methods that we've already described, there are two additional techniques for coaching your child in more complex social skills. These teaching methods involve problem solving and role play.

Problem solving involves brainstorming as many possible solutions to a problem as possible and then choosing solutions or combinations of solutions that are most likely to work. Brainstorming can be great fun. For any particular social problem, there are many possible solutions. When you brainstorm with your child you do not need to worry about how silly or successful different ideas are likely to be. The aim is get as many different possible responses as possible.

For example, imagine a situation in which your child is unfairly accused by the teacher of talking in class when he or she did not do this. Together with your child you make a list of the possible actions that your child could take. Here is one possible list that you might produce when brainstorming:

- shout at the teacher that he or she did not do it

- explain calmly to the teacher that he or she did not do it

- keep quiet and say nothing

- tell the teacher who it was

- wait until the end of the class and then explain to the teacher that he or she did not do it

- storm out of the class crying

- sit quietly and cry

- tell a parent after school

At this stage it's fine to have some really silly suggestions and some that clearly would not be very successful. Talk about each solution and about what might happen if your child tried each of these responses, and work out the advantages and disadvantages of the various alternatives. Then help your child to decide which solution is likely to produce the best results. In some instances your child might decide that a combination of different solutions would be best, rather than just one of the actions.

One thing that we've found to be helpful is to ask children to watch their classmates carefully to work out how these other young people deal with different situations. For example, you could ask your child to discover successful ways that his or her classmates use to join in with group activities. This "investigating" approach can be used to find solutions to many different social challenges.

Role play involves creating an imaginary situation in which you and your child act out a scenario. The idea is for your child to practice his or her social skills in an attempt to deal with a pretend situation. In role play, you both pretend that a particular situation is actually taking place. The aim in role play is to make things as realistic as possible. Before children can start to practice in real-life situations, it's best for them to practice in the safety of home, with someone they trust (you).

Here are some examples of situations that you can role-play with your child. In the more complex situations, you may need to problem-solve the scenario first. Write down each of these scenarios to role-play with your child.

- **Starting a conversation.** A new student starts in your child's class. You decide to ask him or her what his or her name is and where he or she comes from. (Parent plays the part of the new student.)

- **Starting a conversation.** The teacher asks you to do an errand with a student who you don't know very well. You have to walk over to the school office together. (Parent plays the part of the other child.)

- **Maintaining a conversation.** You start at a new school and are sitting in the playground. Another student comes over and sits down in the next seat and asks you how you like the school. You have to answer and then ask a question. (Parent plays the part of the other child.)

- **Asking to join in.** The teacher instructs all the children in the class to find a group and help in producing a poster for the school open house. You look around and the other kids have already gone into groups. Problem-solve how you might go about joining in one of the groups. Role-play how you might approach a group of classmates to ask to join in. (Parent plays the part of another child in the group.)

- **Asking for information.** A parent tells you to go into the local store and buy some tomato sauce. You can't find it and have to ask the shop assistant where it's kept. (Parent plays the part of the shopkeeper.)

- **Asking for information.** You don't hear what the teacher says when he or she gives an instruction in class. You have to ask the teacher to repeat the instruction. (Parent plays the part of the teacher.)

- **Offering help.** A classmate drops his or her homework papers all over the ground and you decide to offer to help pick them up. (Parent plays the part of the other child.)

- **Giving a compliment.** You want to give a compliment to the student sitting in the next seat in class. The other child has done some really excellent art work. (Parent plays the part of the other child.)

- **Offering an invitation.** You have won a couple of free tickets to go to the movies. Problem-solve with how you might invite someone from your class to go along to the movies. Then role-play the chosen response. (Parent plays the part of the other child.)

- **Offering an invitation.** You have a birthday party coming up. Brainstorm how you might go about inviting some classmates or other children. Then role-play how to offer the invitation. (Parent plays the part of classmate[s].)

- **Offering help.** A classmate has forgotten his or her lunch and you decide to offer half of your sandwich. (Parent plays the role of the child who has forgotten the lunch.)

- **Owning up.** You borrow a ball from a kid on your street and then lose it. Brainstorm possible solutions to this problem and decide upon the best solution. Imagine that you decide to tell the other child about having lost the ball and explain that you have bought a new ball to replace it. Role-play this situation. (Parent plays the part of the other kid.)

- **Apologizing.** You drop your parents' favorite plate in the kitchen and it breaks. You're clearing up the bits when your parent walks in. Brainstorm this situation and work out the best solution. Imagine that you decide to apologize to your parent(s) and role-play this scenario. (Parent plays the part of the parent.)

- **Asking for information.** Your teacher assigns some work in class and you do not understand what you're supposed to do. Brainstorm different solutions to this problem. You wait behind after class and ask the teacher to explain. (Parent plays the part of the teacher.)

- **Saying "no."** Another kid is trying to convince you to lend them your favorite possession. You're worried that he or she will break it, and you know that you should say no. (Parent plays the part of the child trying to borrow the item.)

- **Sticking up for yourself.** Your parent accuses you of breaking a window, but you didn't do it. Brainstorm possible solutions to this problem and decide upon the best solution. Imagine that you decide to explain that you did not do it. Role-play this situation. (Parents play the part of themselves in this situation.)

- **Dealing with teasing.** Another child keeps teasing you and calling you mean names. Brainstorm different possible solutions and then role-play the chosen solution. (Parent plays the role of the child doing the teasing.) Parents note: The optimal solution for dealing with teasing will differ for different children. In some instances, a child might handle the situation by teasing back again. Others might be more successful by explaining to the other child or children how hurt he or she is by the teasing. Asking a parent or teacher for help might be the preferred solution for some children. The choice of "best" solution will be for you and your child to work out together.

- **Dealing with bullying.** Another child has been picking on you at school. The bully kicks you whenever he or she walks past. The bully has been taking your lunch and eating it, and going into your school bag and stealing various items. Brainstorm different solutions to this problem and work out which solution is most likely to work. Then role-play how you might handle this situation. (Parent plays the role of the bully.) Parents note: As with teasing, there are no set rules as to how best to deal with bullying. Most schools have antibullying policies and no child should have to tolerate being bullied. Definite action is needed, and if your child is not able to handle the situation him or herself, then it's important that parents and/or teachers intervene. In most instances of bullying, we suggest a combined approach in which the teachers take action at school to reduce the bullying behavior of the bully, while at the same time encouraging the "bullied" child to develop a more assertive approach to the problem. We suggest that parents inform the school immediately if they discover that their child is being bullied. It helps if parents present the problem in a calm manner and in a way that allows the teachers to work in collaboration with both sets of children and parents (the giver and the receiver of the bullying). Some of the different responses that may help in dealing with bullying include ignoring (where possible), informing a teacher or parent, avoiding the bully, staying close to teachers during recess, explaining that such behavior is unacceptable and will be reported, and learning physical defensive methods. Each child needs to work out what tactic will be likely to work for him or her.

Giving Feedback and Praise

When children are learning new skills, they only improve if they're given feedback about whether their performance is correct, or whether some changes need to be made. When children start to practice their new skills, they may not be very competent at first. It's really important that you look for good things in their performance and give them plenty of praise for trying. They must not feel as if they failed. In particular, you need to focus on the good things about your child's performance and tell them what they did well (e.g. "That was a great try. I really liked the way you smiled when you told me your name"). If you're giving feedback about something that needs improvement, this needs to be phrased in a gentle and encouraging way. For example, if your child is not making eye contact during a conversation you could say, "Well done. I really liked the questions you asked. Now try that again and see if you can look at me just a little."

Practicing in the Real World

Once children are able to use their new social skills at home in practice sessions, then they need to practice them in real-life situations. It's important that you set some small homework tasks for real-life practice after each session. However, these tasks need to be simple and relatively easy to perform. There's no point in children trying something far too hard and then failing miserably. They will not be likely to try again in the future, and their worst fears will have come true. You might want to talk to your child's teacher and explain to him or her about the program you're doing. The teacher might have some good ideas about very simple social tasks that your child could try. She or he might even organize some small group situations for your child, where practice will be easier.

Some real-life tasks in which to practice specific body language or voice skills could include:

- saying good morning to the teacher

- saying hello to a particular child (preferably pick a sociable, friendly child to begin with)

- ask a question of a relative when he or she comes to visit

- practice asking questions with a brother or sister

- ask a particular child what their favorite TV show is

- ask a particular child whether he or she has any pets

It's a good idea to organize these practices into a stepladder, just like you're doing with your child's feared situations (see chapter 6).

Only one task should be set after each home practice session. It's helpful to write down the task on a card. The card should describe exactly what the task is, with whom, where, and when it is to be performed. Then, the card should have a space to record when the task was completed and any difficulties that occurred. The practice cards can be used with most children over the age of seven, depending upon reading and writing abilities. With very young children, you may need to prompt the practice of skills by attending playgroups or activities with them.

It's also a good idea to prepare children for ways of handling situations in the event that they don't work out well. For example, it can be devastating to ask to join into a group for the first time, only to be rejected by the group. You need to prepare children to use their realistic thinking to handle things if their early attempts are not very successful. It's also important for you to help children set realistic goals that are within their capabilities. Many anxious children will be only too ready to interpret a reasonable attempt as a failure. If possible, you may want to ask the help of a teacher who can prompt your child on the first couple of occasions. Teachers may also be able to observe from a distance and increase the chance of a successful outcome by discreetly arranging the situation.

Putting Social Skills and Anxiety Management Skills Together

Once children begins to practice their skills in real-life situations, it's important to remember that this part of the social skills program should fit together with the anxiety management methods that they've learned, including relaxation and reality testing. In many cases, learning to deal with new social situations can be regarded as part of your child's fear stepladder. Your child should not be pushed to tackle a difficult social situation when it's still too difficult for him or her. If a particular social situation is still too difficult, remember to break this goal down into smaller, simpler steps. In addition, many of the reality testing exercises that you and your child have planned will include various social contacts. It's very important to remind your child to use these opportunities to practice his or her social skills.

When children are tackling a difficult new situation, you need to remind them to put their skills together. The three R's can be a useful way to help you and your child to remember:

- Relaxation

- Realistic Thinking

- Really Good Social Skills

Creating Social Opportunities

In addition to teaching social skills, parents can help by setting up opportunities for children to practice their social skills. Anxious children often avoid places, such as parties or clubs, where children have the chance to interact with each other. For example, many anxious children protest at the thought of going to a social or activity club, church groups, study groups, chess clubs, or sports clubs. It's a good idea to make a list of all of the social clubs and activities for young people in your area. Your local town council office might be able to help you. Together with your child you can work out which club or activity would be of greatest interest. You may find quite a bit of resistance to the idea from your child. However, it is really worth encouraging your child to attend events where he or she is with other children. You might be able to help by arranging contacts with another family whose child belongs to the particular group. Remember, if it seems too frightening for your child to do this, then it is a useful thing to do. Create a stepladder with the club or group at the top and break it down into smaller steps.

In Summary

The main points presented in this chapter include:

- Social skills are important in allowing children to be successful in their relationships with other children and adults.

- Body language, conversation skills, friendship skills, and assertiveness will help your child to develop successful relationships with others.

- In teaching social skills you need to:
  - stick to one skill at a time
  - keep the sessions short
  - make the sessions fun
  - give feedback in a positive way
  - ensure regular practice
  - allow plenty of time to learn the skills
  - set easy tasks that are likely to be successful first
  - adapt teaching methods to the age of your child

- • refer to a professional therapist when needed
- • Social skills training methods include:
    - • giving instructions
    - • practicing the skills using cue cards and roleplay
    - • giving careful feedback and praise
    - • practicing in real-life situations
    - • creating social opportunities

Chapter 8

Taking Stock

In this chapter we will:

- summarize the techniques that we've covered so far

- go over how these techniques can be put together into a package for your child

- help you decide where to go from here

In the preceding chapters, we took you through a number of techniques or strategies to help your child manage his or her anxiety. Up to this point in our program these strategies have been discussed one at a time, almost as though they are separate. Of course, this is not the case, and we've tried throughout the book to point out where and how your child should be combining strategies in his or her attempts to master anxiety. Even so, don't feel bad if you don't yet completely understanding how the various strategies fit together—it can be tricky.

In this chapter we will first briefly summarize what we have covered in the earlier chapters of this book. Then we will discuss how the various strategies fit together and how they can be combined into a comprehensive program to help your child. We will illustrate this by looking at the specific programs that we planned for the four children who we introduced at the beginning of this book. Finally, we will discuss the future—where you might go from here and what to do if your child once again begins to show signs of excessive fear and anxiety.

What We've Covered So Far

In the opening sections of the book, we discussed what anxiety is and how you can recognize anxiety and fear in your child. We also discussed ways in which your child can learn to understand more about his or her feelings. Hopefully, you were able to use the exercises to teach your child about the three features of anxiety: physical feelings, mental activity, and behaviors. We also introduced the idea of recording your child's anxiety using our 10-point worry scale. By this stage, your child should be getting pretty good at rating his or her degree of anxiety and should realize that anxiety varies from situation to situation.

We also explained to you a little of where anxiety might come from, and hopefully this gave you some understanding of why your child might be anxious. At the end of chapter 1, we gave you a model of the things that keep your child anxious in the here and now, and this allowed us to explain to you the various techniques we would cover. These techniques included relaxation, realistic thinking, reality testing, and the building of social skills.

Relaxation involves teaching your child how to reduce muscle tension and feel more physically relaxed in frightening situations. The main technique we taught involves tensing and relaxing different muscle groups in turn.

The following points were made:

- Relaxation is a skill that your child has to learn and practice.

- Relaxation practice needs to become a regular habit.

- With children, relaxation sessions need to be short and simple.

- Regular practice will help your child to use his or her relaxation skills in real life.

Realistic thinking is used to help your child change his or her current ways of thinking about frightening situations. We suggested that anxious children (and adults) tend to think unrealistically and regularly look at the negative in situations. In particular, anxious children overestimate how likely it will be that bad things will happen and catastrophize about how bad those things will be. We showed you exercises to help your child realize that his or her feelings could be changed if he or she could learn to think differently about situations. Most importantly, your child was taught to think like a detective and look for evidence regarding his or her beliefs. The following points were made:

- It's your thoughts and beliefs that directly cause your feelings in a situation.

- Worried thoughts cause you to feel more anxious. Calm thoughts cause you to feel more relaxed.

- You need to act like a detective in frightening situations and look for evidence for your worried thoughts.

- There are many types of evidence you can look for. Some of the best sources of evidence come from previous experience and other explanations.

Reality testing is the crucial technique. It involves encouraging your child to face up to his or her fears. Reality testing is most likely to work when it's consistent and systematic. There are several steps to reality testing:

- Brainstorm all of the situations your child fears and avoids.

- Group them together into similar or related fears.

- Organize the fears and create small steps so that your child has a series of stepladders.

- Your child should begin with the first step of each ladder and gradually work his or her way up the ladder.

- Each successful attempt at a step should be rewarded.

There are also several points to increase the chance that reality testing will work:

- Make sure steps are not too far apart.

- Repeat each step several times until your child is more or less bored with it.

- To keep your child's motivation going, rewards need to be given when promised and as soon as possible after the step.

- Rewards should also be the right size for the particular step.

Finally, we discussed your child's social skills, or the way your child interacts with other people. Many anxious children have no problems with social skills, and if this is true for your child, this component can be left out of your child's program. But if your child does lack some social skills, it's important to address this in order to give your child as many positive experiences as possible.

We described a number of exercises you could use with your child to help him or her understand more about how to develop various social skills. When teaching your child social skills, we suggested the following points:

- Teach one skill at a time.

- Make the lessons fun and keep them short.

- You need to give your child feedback about his or her current ways of acting and then show him or her a better way to act.

- Your child will need lots of practice.

- Begin with the more basic skills and gradually build to more difficult ones.

Finally, don't forget the chapter on child management skills. In this chapter we discussed the ways in which you might accidentally increase your child's anxiety and ways in which you can better handle your child's anxiety. Some of the main points we made were as follows:

- Protecting or taking over for your child may make him or her feel better in the short run, but this will maintain his or her anxiety over time.

- It's more useful to encourage your child to face fears.

- If children ask for help, you can help best by guiding them in how to solve the problem and then encouraging them to do it themselves.

- If children regularly ask for reassurance, you should guide them in how to solve the problem (e.g. realistic thinking) and then let them know that you will ignore further requests for help.

- Remember to reward your child for behaviors that you're happy with.

- If you find it difficult to let your child make his or her own mistakes, you need to do realistic thinking yourself to convince yourself that your child will not suffer in the long run if things do not always go right.

Some Sample Programs

Using every one of these techniques and components is not always necessary for each child. Some types of problems need certain techniques more than others, and some children will find that some techniques make more sense for them than others. Therefore, even though it's important for you and your child to understand all of these techniques, you may find that the program you and your child choose does not necessarily use each of the techniques we have covered. We will now revisit the four children we've mentioned throughout this book and describe the final program each of them selected. You will notice that the most essential technique that each of them does include is the reality testing. Your child will not learn to master his or her fears if he or she does not do lots of reality testing practice.

Talia

You may remember that Talia had a fear of water. Overall, she was a confident, outgoing nine-year-old, but Talia was afraid of swimming, and this was starting to affect her confidence with friends.

In this type of case, where the problem is very restricted and the child is not generally shy or sensitive, the program can be a very quick and straightforward one that involves only reality testing. Talia's program, therefore, began with Talia and her parents brainstorming all sorts of situations that made Talia afraid. They then organized these situations into a stepladder—from easiest to hardest. Because Talia's fear was a very specific one, it was quite easy to come up with a lot of steps that very gradually got harder and harder. Also, because Talia really wanted to get over her problem and go swimming with her friends, her parents only had to use a few small rewards from time to time to get her to do her practice. Most of the time, they just needed to remind her of her final goal—going to the beach with her friends. The whole program for Talia only took around three weeks and, before long, Talia's fear of water was far behind her.

George

George had a much broader and more general problem than Talia. He was a boy who was shy and sensitive and had little self-confidence. Because of his fears, George avoided many social interactions and had few friends. He also had times of feeling low.

Because George's fears were very much focused on the way he thought about things, and because he was an intelligent young man, George's parents decided to focus strongly on the realistic thinking component of the program. They spent a great deal of time working on getting George to think more realistically about his abilities, and most importantly about what other people thought of him. The most important lessons that George needed to learn were: you can do things well; even if you do something badly, other people will not necessarily think badly of you; and even if they do, it is not the end of the world, and those people are simply not a suitable match for you. George did well with his lessons, but they were hard ones to really believe. He did begin to shift his beliefs, but they did not change completely.

To try and really reinforce these new beliefs, George's parents included reality testing into his program. Because George was so unconfident and also a little depressed, he really needed lots of encouragement and motivation to work on what were some pretty difficult tasks. So George's parents made sure that the reality testing stepladders had lots of very small steps and that they gave George lots of rewards and encouragement along the way. This meant that George's program took quite a long time—in fact, it became a way of life that George and his parents continued to some extent for many years. But by making sure that the steps were small enough that George managed to do them on most occasions, George was able to have plenty of successes and lots of rewards and encouragement from his parents, which slowly but surely began to boost George's confidence.

Finally, while doing his reality testing, it became clear to George's parents that he really did lack a few basic skills and the ability to really get along with other kids. This was very understandable given that George had had hardly any friends over the years. In his first year of high school, George was also starting to be teased by a few of the kids. So George's parents made sure that they also included some work on George's social skills in his program. George and his parents practiced different ways of meeting new kids and of talking to kids. George then made sure that he practiced these new skills during his reality testing and in his daily life. Because the teasing was not too severe, George didn't want his parents to talk to the school teachers about it. Instead, he practiced ways of dealing with the teasing, especially trying to let the kids know that he was okay with their comments and that they didn't bother him. Luckily, this seemed to be enough, and the teasing stopped after a short while. This success was a huge boost for George's confidence.

George is still working on his anxiety and it will be a long-term task for him. But over the course of several weeks, he was already a very different boy than the one who began the program. As George's confidence began to build, his depression also became less of an issue. George and his parents were happy with the changes and didn't feel that he needed to do any special work on his earlier low moods.

Lashi

Lashi was a young girl whose parents had separated. She worried that her mother might be injured or killed and that she would never see her again. As a result, she became upset whenever she had to separate from her mother. Because Lashi was only seven, her mother decided that the realistic thinking might be too hard for her. Instead, she decided to focus on teaching Lashi to relax. This also fitted with her mother's general philosophy in life since she herself had done several relaxation courses over the years.

Lashi really enjoyed the relaxation, especially because it gave her some special time alone with her mother. She never really learned to completely relax, but she was able to do enough that it gave her the start that she needed before moving on to reality testing.

The main part of the program for Lashi was the reality testing. Lashi and her mother worked out a number of stepladders for different sections of her problem—going to school, staying overnight at other people's houses, being left with a sitter, and so on. Each ladder was broken down into small steps and Lashi picked some fun rewards for doing each one. Many of the rewards involved special time with her mother. Part of the program also involved Lashi's mother not allowing Lashi to ask for too much reassurance.

Lashi's mother also realized that the separation had affected her in many ways. Most importantly, she realized that following the breakup of the relationship, she became extra scared of losing Lashi. As a result, she had started to be a little too protective of Lashi and was perhaps a bit too forgiving of her fears. Lashi's mother had to admit that sometimes when she let Lashi stay home from school, she really didn't mind too much. So Lashi's mother decided to work on being a little less protective and to be tougher in encouraging Lashi to face her fears. As part of this change, Lashi's mother began to do some realistic thinking for her own worries: What would really happen if Lashi became a little scared? Would Lashi really hate her if she made Lashi go to school? And so on.

Finally, when Lashi was doing pretty well in separating from her mother, she and her mother worked out another stepladder for Lashi's other fears of injections and hospitals.

Kurt

Kurt had two main problems—repetitive washing because of a fear of germs, and a more generalized anxiety that affected all sorts of different areas. Because of the complexity of these problems, Kurt's first step was to be very clear about all of the behaviors and features that went with each type of difficulty. Kurt labeled his anxieties his "washing problem" and his "worry problem" so that he could keep them straight in his head. There was a lot of similarity in the two problems, but there were also some differences that Kurt needed to be clear on.

Kurt's father was not interested in helping, but he and his mother worked on the program together. They began by working on realistic thinking. For his washing problem, Kurt needed to learn that he was not picking up lots of germs and that even if he was, they would not hurt him. For his worry problem, Kurt needed to learn the general rule that the world was not a particularly dangerous place, and that he was not especially likely to get hurt. Because there were so many things that Kurt worried about, it was quite easy to think of lots of evidence to prove to himself that he was not thinking realistically. Kurt was able to begin to use his detective, James Bond, to help him through some tough situations.

As for all programs, Kurt also included reality testing. The reality testing for Kurt was a little harder to think of because the worries were so much less concrete. But, by thinking hard, Kurt and his mother were able to come up with several stepladders and lots of steps. Remember that we gave you some examples for these types of problems in chapter 6. The hard part for Kurt came especially when he had to go through several days without washing. But his determination and the rewards his mother used helped him get through it. After many weeks, it began to get easier.

Where Do You Go from Here?

Congratulations—you've reached the end of the program. If you and your child have followed through the lessons in this book carefully, it has probably been a long, hard road. Hopefully, it has also been a worthwhile one. Your son or daughter should be quite a different child from the one who started this program. But, of course, everyone is different, and how much your child has changed will depend on so many things.

Probably the main questions on your mind now are: Where do we go from here? How long do we keep practicing and when can we put all this behind us and forget all about it? These questions unfortunately don't have a clear-cut answer. Every child is different and every situation varies. We've treated some children who make huge gains in a few short weeks and never look back. Others might change slowly and to only a small degree, and they may really need to keep going with their practice for months or even years. The typical child is probably somewhere in between. They may practice hard for ten to twenty weeks and make good changes. At this point, they can stop doing set, formal practices, but they and their parents need to keep in mind all that they have learned for the rest of their lives. They need to keep reminding themselves of the principles of realistic thinking and reality testing and, whenever they get a chance, they should do the occasional practice. This doesn't mean having to do formal practice, it simply means to practice whenever life throws something a little tough your child's way. For example, when your child has exams, or a big sporting event, or perhaps has to give a speech at an awards night, these are chances for your child to remind him or herself of the techniques he or she has learned. If she or he finds that anxiety is high, it's a chance to practice the techniques properly again for a week or so, just to get back on top of things. The practice your child has to do shouldn't be too painful over time because many of the techniques should become a natural and normal part of his or her life. As your child builds confidence, makes new friends, and has successes, the techniques such as realistic thinking, social skills, and even reality testing will be something that he or she does as an everyday part of living.

Our last point is to raise the possibility of what professionals call "relapse." There is a possibility that, at some point, your child will once again begin to experience problems with excessive fears and anxiety. This is not necessarily going to happen and, for many children, it never does. But if you remember back to chapter 1, you know that genetically your child is a sensitive child, and so there's always the possibility that anxiety will once again rear its head.

This may happen for a number of reasons. First, once life starts to feel good again it's understandable that children and their parents often stop practicing their techniques. Sometimes, in these cases, anxiety just has a habit of very gradually creeping back. Second, bad things do happen in life. Your child may lose someone close to him or her, or he or she could fail an important exam, lose a close friend, or be in a car accident. When something bad happens in life, it makes many of us begin to think for a while that dangers are very likely. In the case of sensitive children, this might be enough to bring back the negative thoughts and feelings of anxiety. Finally, anxiety and fears can return in some cases during times of general stress. For example, if you or your partner become unemployed, or you have a burglary, or you separate, these general stresses that enter the family and affect all of you may cause your child to lose confidence and begin to have fears again.

If relapse does happen, it's not something to panic over. Simply going back to basics and practicing the techniques that worked the first time should get things under control quickly. When your child's return of fear has been triggered by another problem such as stress in the family or a major calamity, it's important to allow all of you time to deal with that stress first. For example, let's imagine that your partner lands in hospital after a serious work accident and the whole family is distressed. Your child might lose some confidence, and you might find that some of the fears that she or he had before, or even some new ones, might develop. It's important not to immediately start to do realistic thinking, reality testing, and so on, in a frantic fashion. Rather, allow everyone time to adjust to the changes in your life and deal with the practical problems and the emotions of the situation first. Once you are starting to get a little control over the stress in your life, then you can begin to practice the anxiety control techniques again.

An important point to remember is that if your child does show some signs of anxiety again, it will take much less time the second time around to get on top of them. Your child should now know the techniques well and will be able to put them straight into practice. In addition, the anxiety will not have had so long to take hold.

We certainly hope that nothing terrible does happen in your child's life and that he or she manages to live a life free of interference from anxiety. But even if there are difficulties along the road, it's good to know that your child has now learned some techniques and skills that will be of benefit through the rest of his or her life.

Ronald M. Rapee, Ph.D., is a professor in the Department of Psychology at Macquarie University in Sydney, Australia.

Susan H. Spence, Ph.D., is a professor of psychology at the University of Queensland in Brisbane, Australia.

Vanessa Cobham, Ph.D., is a lecturer in the Department of Psychology at the University of Queensland in Brisbane.

Ann Wignall, M. Psych., is a clinical psychologist with the Department of Child and Adolescent Psychiatry of Royal North Shore Hospital in Sydney.

Some Other
New Harbinger Titles

Helping Your Depressed Child, Item 3228 $14.95

The Couples's Guide to Love and Money, Item 3112 $18.95

50 Wonderful Ways to be a Single-Parent Family, Item 3082 $12.95

Caring for Your Grieving Child, Item 3066 $14.95

Helping Your Child Overcome an Eating Disorder, Item 3104 $16.95

Helping Your Angry Child, Item 3120 $17.95

The Stepparent's Survival Guide, Item 3058 $17.95

Drugs and Your Kid, Item 3015 $15.95

The Daughter-In-Law's Survival Guide, Item 2817 $12.95

Whose Life Is It Anyway?, Item 2892 $14.95

It Happened to Me, Item 2795 $17.95

Act it Out, Item 2906 $19.95

Parenting Your Older Adopted Child, Item 2841 $16.95

Boy Talk, Item 271X $14.95

Talking to Alzheimer's, Item 2701 $12.95

Helping a Child with Nonverbal Learning Disorder or Asperger's Syndrome, Item 2779 $14.95

The 50 Best Ways to Simplify Your Life, Item 2558 $11.95

When Anger Hurts Your Relationship, Item 2604 $13.95

The Couple's Survival Workbook, Item 254X $18.95

Loving Your Teenage Daughter, Item 2620 $14.95

The Hidden Feeling of Motherhood, Item 2485 $14.95

Parenting Well When You're Depressed, Item 2515 $17.95

Thinking Pregnant, Item 2302 $13.95

Call **toll free, 1-800-748-6273,** or log on to our online bookstore at **www.newharbinger.com** to order. Have your Visa or Mastercard number ready. Or send a check for the titles you want to New Harbinger Publications, Inc., 5674 Shattuck Ave., Oakland, CA 94609. Include $4.50 for the first book and 75¢ for each additional book, to cover shipping and handling. (California residents please include appropriate sales tax.) Allow two to five weeks for delivery.

Prices subject to change without notice.